Deanna Morgan Kirby

Just Crazy to ski

A Fifty-Year History of Skiing at Los Alamos

Los Alamos Historical Society
Los Alamos, New Mexico
2003

Library of Congress Cataloging-in-Publication Data

Kirby, Deanna Morgan.
Just crazy to ski : a fifty-year history of skiing at Los Alamos / Deanna Morgan Kirby.
p. cm.
Includes bibliographical references (p.).
ISBN 0-941232-32-8 (pbk.)
1. Los Alamos Ski Club--History. 2. Skis and skiing--New Mexico--Pajarito Mountain--History. 3. Pajarito Mountain (N.M.) I. Title.
GV854.A1K57 2003
796.93'09789'58--dc22
2003065831

Cover photo: Becky Bradford (later Becky Diven) demonstrates a snowplow turn at Sawyer's Hill.

Permission to print excerpts from Edith Warner's 1945 Christmas letter (pages 40 and 41) granted by the family of Edith Warner.

The word Pajarito, pronounced Pa-ha-REE-tow, means "little bird" in Spanish. The little bird that appears at the end of each section was drawn by Bob Mills, a long-time resident of Los Alamos and a skier. The little bird appeared on the ski passes at one time.

Los Alamos Historical Society
P.O. Box 43
Los Alamos, New Mexico 87544

Printed in the United States of America
Printed by Starline Printing, Albuquerque, New Mexico

Contents

Foreword

Ed Cort

Just Crazy to Ski, Deanna Morgan Kirby's book about Pajarito* Mountain and the Los Alamos Ski Club, begins with the story of building the atomic bomb during World War II. It combines this with another epic struggle: to build and operate a ski area that operates as a non-profit corporation, offering instruction, equipment, and uphill facilities to skiers at nominal cost.

For the most part, ski areas like Pajarito that are owned and operated by private clubs reflect a simpler era, when skiing was a family affair-leather boots, bamboo poles, wool mittens drying around a base lodge wood stove. Although they are seen less often now, these images still persist at Pajarito, whose simple family-oriented skiing experience is fostered by the management. Today's economics have been hard on small family-oriented ski areas like Pajarito, and only a few club-owned and club-operated areas survive. The ones that remain occupy a unique rung on the American ski ladder. Fickle weather, bad national economy, and competition from massive resorts has meant the loss of 400 of these small "feeder" ski areas in the past 15 years according to the October 1993 issue of Powder magazine.

Articles in magazines and local newspapers love to have fun with Pajarito's "secret" image. Although highly exaggerated, the stories contain a grain of truth about the image. First, the magazine writers enjoy tying the laboratory's secret wartime role and its continuing military research mission with the ski area's low-key profile. Of course, there is no connection. Second, it is true that the ski area was built by and for the (mostly) Ph.D. physicists, chemists, engineers, and others associated with the Manhattan Project and its successors. As described by one of them, nuclear chemist Rene Prestwood, in the November 1991 issue of Ski magazine, "We had a great spirit of adventure, of creating something. None of us were rich and we were used to working hard. The town was always kind of isolated so we put our energy into skiing." Pajarito Mountain's main lodge is named the "Bob Thorn" lodge in memory of Harvard-trained physicist Robert N. Thorn, who rose through the ranks to become acting director of the Los Alamos National Laboratory. The lodge is named in recognition of his dedication and leadership in building Pajarito Mountain and not for his scientific or management roles at

---

*Pajarito, pronounced Pa-ha-REE-tow, means "little bird" in Spanish.

the Laboratory, which were also legendary. The photos that Kirby has collected for this book, and those on display in the Bob Thorn lodge, document the endless hours of dedicated volunteers cutting trees, rolling rocks, stacking and burning slash, planning budgets, and meeting in committees over the fifty-year period described in this book.

The real reason for the secret image is that the Los Alamos Ski Club is a non-profit organization. If the club advertises or promotes Pajarito, it could appear to be in competition with New Mexico's commercial ski operators-and incur the wrath of the IRS. Under tax rules, the ski area cannot be in competition with other areas, so Pajarito bends over backward to maintain its non-competitive relationship.

When my family arrived in Los Alamos in late summer 1972, almost the first thing we did was drive our rental car to the ski area base for a look. After catching our breath, we drove immediately to the "Lemon Lot," the town's informal used car parking spot where buyers and sellers arrange their own deals. We bought a 1963 International Scout with four-wheel drive and limited slip differential; the "Yellow Submarine" our boys called it, because it dripped with condensation from snow-covered skiers on the way back down the hill each ski day. That winter of 1972–73 it snowed 8 inches on Halloween Night in White Rock, and the ski lifts started a week before Thanksgiving. They didn't stop until May 5, and snow storms arrived every Thursday or Friday like clockwork.

Besides providing access to skiing, the lifts also provide beautiful views of the Sangre de Cristo Mountains across the Rio Grande Valley far below to the east. In the valley are the sacred Black Mesa and Indian pueblos that were inhabited long before Columbus set sail. There's not so much secrecy as mystery in that view. From the top of the chairlifts, you can peer into the Valle Grande, the peaceful center of what was once a volcano's cauldron. Just standing there on the Valle rim, on a clear winter morning, is enough to make your heart soar—like a Pajarito.

Deanna Kirby has given us a priceless look at the times and the spirit of the people who built Pajarito Mountain. Unlike many other ski areas—built by wealthy individuals, corporations, or government entities—Pajarito Mountain's story shows how a group of (not quite so) ordinary individuals, working together, can accomplish much. In that way, Pajarito Mountain Ski area's story is typical of America's experience.

Introduction

Over the fifty-year history covered in this book, the Los Alamos Ski Club story has been enriched by history and place, but the ideas, plans, energy, and enthusiasm from the people add form, color, and texture to its substance. As memories of the volunteers lend voice to the story, their labor created the reality of a ski area, first at Sawyer's Hill and finally at Pajarito Mountain.

Today, Pajarito Mountain represents not only a splendid recreational area but is a shining tribute to the volunteers and the successes of their labor. Imbued with camaraderie and a passion to ski, the volunteer spirit is the heart and soul of the Los Alamos Ski Club story.

When I began this project, the task seemed overwhelming. But once again the spirit of volunteerism was alive and well as people stepped forward to share their time, their stories, their pictures, and their expertise to help me write the history of skiing in Los Alamos. The Los Alamos Ski Club granted me access to all of its records. The reader should know that without the original ski club newsletters and videotapes of "old timers" recorded in the mid-1980s, piecing together the early history of the ski club would have been impossible. The interviews of key players in the Los Alamos ski history were the brainchild of Paul Allison, James "Stretch" Fretwell, and Dale Holm, who had the foresight to videotape and preserve these oral histories. In addition, I conducted many, many interviews of people who played a role in this history. Other long-time residents granted me access to their personal letters and records. I relied on the archives of the Los Alamos Historical Society, as well as a number of the books published by the society.

This book does not attempt to cover every aspect of ski history in Los Alamos; for example, while I mention the ski instructors and the ski patrol, I have not gone in-depth into their history—that would require another book. Nor do I mention the ski and skate sale, the annual effort to make ski passes, or the work that went into repairing chain saws, even though this work was all done by volunteers. Nor do I attempt to cover the early years of skiing during the Ranch School era other than with a few photographs and captions. I focused on the period between 1943 and 1993 and on the effort needed to shape the development of the ski areas at Sawyer's Hill and Pajarito Mountain.

I so appreciate the critique and suggestions of the following people who read all or parts of the book: Becky and Ben Diven, Perc King, John Rogers, Ron Strong, and the Senior Citizens Writing Group. I am grateful to the Los Alamos Historical Society for its willingness to publish the book, and to the members of the Publications Committee for their comments and suggestions. I am indebted to the support and volunteer efforts of Kyle Wheeler, editor, and Gloria Sharp, designer. I am forever grateful to the patient support of my husband, Bob, who helped collect photographs, sat through most of the interviews, and read the manuscript many times. From the depth of my heart, I thank all who have shared in this book. May the spirit of volunteerism endure.

The title of the book comes from a comment made during an interview I did of Perc King. As he described one event after another, he paused and said enthusiastically, "We were just so crazy to ski!" At that moment, I knew I had a title for my book. I hope you enjoy it.

Deanna Morgan Kirby
2003

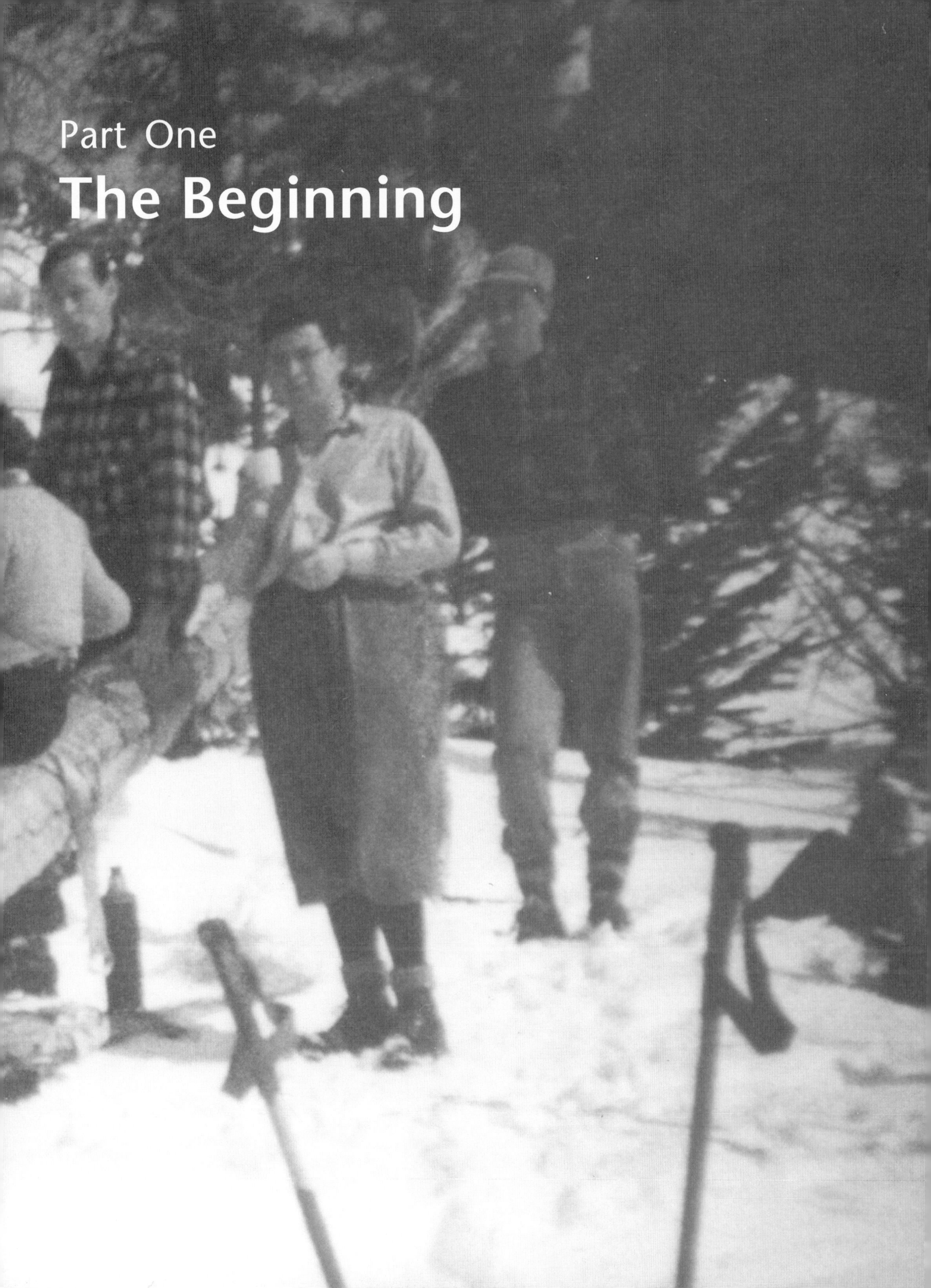

Part One

The Beginning

The Hill

From top: The Big House—the school dormitory for the Ranch School and a library and post exchange during Manhattan Project days—was torn down in 1948; the Jemez Mountains to the west of Fuller Lodge, with the Ranch School gardens in the foreground; students of the Ranch School enjoyed skiing, despite beginning each run with a strenuous climb.

In 1942, war raged around the world, and the United States, with its allies, was locked in battle against Nazi Germany and Japan. To win World War II was the consummate goal that gripped the nation and united its people. Hearts blazed with patriotism, from the soldiers in foxholes defending freedom to the children pledging allegiance to the flag.

Los Alamos, a small community set on the Pajarito Plateau in northern New Mexico, was the site of the exclusive Los Alamos Ranch School for boys, founded in 1917 by Ashley Pond. Because of its remote location, Los Alamos was selected as the site for the super secret Manhattan Project, and the Ranch School was confiscated by the U.S. government one year after the attack on Pearl Harbor. It was an early evening on December 7, 1942, when the faculty and the boys were summoned to the Big House, a three-story log building on the campus with screened porches all around where some of the boys slept. Hugh Church, a grandson of Ashley Pond, recalled that everyone was there. "I remember the telegram being read."

Signed by Secretary of War Henry L. Stimson, the telegram advised the faculty and students "...that it has been determined necessary to the interests of the United States in the prosecution of the War that the property of Los Alamos Ranch School be acquired for military purposes. Therefore... a condemnation proceeding will be instituted."

Director A.J. Connell and the Board of Directors agreed to sell the financially burdened school, perhaps thinking it would return to its original purpose after the war. Shock waves from the cannons of war that destroyed lives and ravaged lands beyond the oceans rocked the quiet mesa and left the school's occupants stunned by the harsh orders from the War Department. They were given two weeks to pack their belongings and vacate the premises.

Reluctantly, the government did allow the Ranch School instructors and students to remain through January to hurriedly complete their semester of studies. Christmas vacation was canceled! Four seniors would be the last to graduate from the historic school. They were Collier W. Baird and Stirling A. Colgate from New Jersey and William Edgar Barr and Theodore Spencer Church, Hugh's brother, from New Mexico.

Within a week, the Army Corps of Engineers brought in bulldozers, graders, and mechanical ditch diggers that noisily swarmed over the mesa, clearing brush and breaking up the frozen ground for a laboratory. "It was like an invasion," said Church, "a mechanized invasion."

The invading Army spared Fuller Lodge, a rustic building constructed of 800 hand-hewn Ponderosa pine logs. Its dining room remained open, and the staff and faculty apartments on the second and third floors were converted to guest rooms. Other Ranch School buildings were also left intact by the Army—the Arts and Crafts Building, which housed the school laboratory; some residences; the Big House; two stone buildings (formerly power houses); the Trading Post; and an old stone icehouse near a small pond later named after Ashley Pond, the Ranch School founder.

Selected for its secluded location, Los Alamos became a secret Army Post encircled by barbed-wire fences and guarded by military police.

General Leslie Richard Groves, a burly man endowed with endless energy and unflinching confidence, had been charged by General Brehon Somervell to direct the Manhattan Engineering District Project, of which Los Alamos was a part. In turn, Groves recommended to the Military Policy Committee that J. Robert Oppenheimer, a lanky, chain-smoking theoretician from Berkeley, California, who had attained respect among his peers for his scientific work, be named director of the new laboratory.

Thus the military establishment and civilian community entered into a wary relationship that reluctantly allowed freedom of information for the scientists yet imposed military-life restrictions upon the inhabitants of the newly formed community.

Parents and friends of the Ranch School boys celebrated a graduation ceremony under the front portico of Fuller Lodge. Indians, dressed in traditional clothing, sometimes danced and sold pottery. Students rode horses year-round.

Rows of laundry, amidst the tar-papered Quonset huts and expandable trailers, add to the chaotic background of a forest of electrical poles and smokestacks. These dwellings represented the least-desired housing during the early years at Los Alamos.

In late spring of 1943, an eclectic mix of military personnel and civilians, leaving behind friends and relatives for the duration of the project, began to settle at Site Y, one of several code names for Los Alamos. The name Los Alamos was not mentioned off the mesa tops—in Washington, it was referred to as the Manhattan District; in Santa Fe, it was called Site Y; the Army called it the Reservation; and to many others, it was simply "the Hill" or "up yonder." The civilians included several Nobel laureates and others who would later receive Nobel prizes. Their new address became P.O. Box 1663, Santa Fe, New Mexico. Their mail was censored. All their guns and cameras had to be checked into the Army vault. Although they could leave the Hill at will with a pass, they were admonished not to fraternize with the locals, nor could they travel beyond Taos, Las Vegas, Albuquerque, or Cuba, New Mexico, without specific permission. Only numbers appeared on drivers licenses, which were not signed, and when a well-known scientist traveled, he assumed a false name. For security reasons, there could be no mention of the words *scientist* or *physicist*, so everyone's occupation was listed as *engineer*.

The opportunity to apply the mysteries of the relatively new science of nuclear physics to the wartime effort induced scientists to abandon teaching posts, lecture podiums, and research grants that had attracted many of them to prestigious colleges and universities.

Engineers, machinists, tool makers, technicians, and others with specialized skills were either assigned to the project through the Army's Special Engineering Detachment (SED) or recruited from industry.

Harlow Russ, who would spend years in Los Alamos, after reading his offer of employment from the War Department, wrote that his first reaction was, "anyone would be crazy to turn down an offer to go to an unknown location to do unspecified work on an unknown war project."

Englishmen from war-torn Britain, as well as Canadians, Swiss, and other nationalities, who had fled oppression in Poland, Hungary, Austria, Italy, and Germany, joined the secret project.*

There were GIs and Wacs. There were families with children, dogs, cats, bicycles, trikes, and toys. The average age of the population was 26. They were bright, some even brilliant, and they were energetic and adventurous.

The average age of the population was 26. They were bright, some even brilliant, and they were energetic and adventurous.

No matter how small their part was in the project—nor how difficult it was to maintain a household on the secret mesa—they

**In the late fall of 1943, members of the British Mission began to arrive in Los Alamos. First came Otto Frisch and E.W. Titterton. They were followed by Rudolf Peierls, William G. Penney, George Placzek, P.B. Moon, James L. Tuck, Egon Bretscher, and Klaus Fuchs, among others. James Chadwick, Geoffrey Taylor, and Niels Bohr and his physicist son, Aage, would often visit Los Alamos as consultants.*

Left: A New Mexico landscape; above: Dorothy McKibbin welcomed newcomers at 109 East Palace Avenue in Santa Fe, first stop after their arrival. She allayed their fears of the unknown and offset disappointments aggravated by exhaustion from long travels.

felt inspired and uplifted. Aware of the drama of their situation, Jane Wilson wrote that they were "buoyed up by the fact that here at Los Alamos, an event of magnitude was being wrought."

Everyday of the week, except Sundays, the scientific community worked long hours, for they were pressured by time. It was critical that they build the atomic bomb before Germany did.

Beauty and Grim Reality

The first stop for this unique breed of pioneers was 109 East Palace Avenue in Santa Fe. Arriving sleepless, tired, and tense with expectancy, they met Dorothy McKibbin, who was charge d'affaires of the Santa Fe office, the hostess and friend who provided newcomers with their first introduction to the Hill. Notified of each person's arrival in advance, she greeted them and passed out yellow maps marked by red pencil, tracing every mile of the route to up yonder. Anxious to complete their trip to their new home, they proceeded either in their own cars, with one of the staff, or on a clunky, gargantuan Army bus that bounced and bumped over the New Mexico roads.

For eyes accustomed to city skyscrapers, farmlands green with crops, or ocean waves breaking onto sandy shores, the southwestern scenery, with its brilliant blue sky and extraordinary vistas, left them

Top: The Laboratory's quickly constructed "Technical Area" around Ashley Pond. Half of a one-story structure, visible in the upper center of the photo, was later used as the first ski lodge at Pajarito Mountain. Middle: Cars stop at the Main Gate for pass inspection when entering or leaving Los Alamos. The author, as a teenager, was once caught trying to sneak through using the badge of a friend. Bottom: An MP checks the badge of a resident.

wide-eyed. Years later, Bernice Brode recalled that, on her first approach to Los Alamos, she felt "bewitched by the stretches of red earth and pink rocks with dark shrubbery scattered along the ocher cliffs, lavender vistas in the distant Sangre de Cristo mountain range."

Though some saw only a hot and barren country with cacti, sage brush, and piñon trees rooted in sand, Italian physicist Emilio Segrè, who would receive a Nobel prize in 1959, described the landscape that had been wrenched from the earth by volcanic activity as "a beautiful and savage country."

"What a superb retreat in which to spend the war years," wrote Brode of the remote region where "all was beauty and quiet." But the grim reality of Site Y was not beauty. Brode described it as "plain, utilitarian, and quite ugly."

The first stop was at the guard's hutment, a bare-bones structure not much larger than the nearby outhouse. Inside the hut, "stark walls were decorated with starkly naked pinup girls," recalled Ruth Marshak, a third-grade teacher. Newcomers were issued temporary passes that had to be shown when entering or leaving the Project. "They were to be a solemn business in our lives. A lost pass meant hours of delay in the guard's hutment."

Once past the guard gate, newcomers encountered Quonset huts covered in tar paper and a squalid trailer camp with green coaches cramped into uniform formations, military tight. Beseiged by bulldozers, noise of hammers pounding, and tangles of looping wires, one resident noted that, "The mesa was a construction camp...all was raw and new."

South of the pond by Los Alamos Canyon was the Technical Area that accommodated the work on the weapon. The buildings, surrounded by a security fence, were in the style of Army barracks and were painted industrial green. In fact, every building on the mesa seemed to be green.

Even the school, built on a foundation blasted from rock, was painted a "bilious green," wrote Marshak. Though the view of the Jemez mountain range seen beyond the school's great plate windows was unexcelled, "the school furnace was subject to idiosyncracies as were the furnaces of our homes...sometimes there was no heat or the furnace blasted and roared...and it struck me as significant, if not symbolic, that in our school the electric clocks occasionally ran backwards."

From top left: The water tank provided a reference point for the fire department and citizens; Spruce Cottage, a typical Bathtub Row home (more than one acrimonious battle was fought to determine who might move to the row); a Sundt apartment building could house four families.

North of Fuller Lodge, the original homes of the Ranch School instructors housed eminent scientists and Army elite. Containing the only bathtubs in town, these charming log-and-stone homes lined a street called Bathtub Row.

Angled among the pines, north and west of the Tech Area, stood two-story, four-unit family dwellings. Built under a contract by the Sundt Corporation, they were called Sundts. Though they were labeled "luxury apartments" and featured hardwood floors and fireplaces, they were painted dull green; their exteriors often appeared unkempt, with coal bins over-flowing; woodpiles were stacked everywhere; laundry flapped from strung clotheslines; garbage pails were often neglected by the collectors; and back staircases were exposed to the street.

Dormitories provided rooms for single men and women.

Yards were without walkways or grass except for some patches of frail, green lawn by Fuller Lodge and the Bathtub Row homes. Kathleen Mark, wife of Canadian theoretician Carson Mark, lamented about the landscape, "Nowhere on the ground was there any sustained greenness."

Dirt streets without names crisscrossed the mesa. Directions to homes were given using the old, shingled water tower, located near Fuller Lodge, as the reference point. Confused by the twist of roads and sameness of the buildings, frustrated firefighters often sped to the wrong location.

Melting snow or summer rains turned roads and yards into gooey quagmires of ankle-deep mud that dried like concrete on soles of shoes and left deep, hardened ruts where vehicles had left their imprints. During the dry season, gusty winds stirred up clouds of fine, gritty dust that sifted into the leaky houses.

Mesa life for these kindred spirits, adjusting to their new environment, often butted against the arbitrary decisions dictated by the Army command. Daily complaints, especially about the commissary, were directed toward the Army, which ran the post.

Consumers griped for months about the lack of fresh eggs. Another major irritation was the shortage of milk (due to the mushrooming population) and its uncertain delivery to the commissary. One group petitioned the commanding officer to raise cash for purchasing local vegetables that would be fresher than those shipped from Texas. However, their worst quarrel with the commissary was its frequent "closing for inventory," wrote Brode.

Mici Teller (wife of Edward Teller, who would later be known as "the father of the hydrogen bomb") complained, "Never in my life have I been acquainted with these inventories. I think they are just having the excuse to all go to Santa Fe."

It was Mici who staged the first sit-in on the Hill. Determined to save backyard trees from the Army plow, she argued with the soldier who had unretractable orders to "level off everything so we can plant it," he said. She told him, "It made no sense as it was planted by wild nature and suited me better than dust."

The first birth in the Los Alamos hospital was in 1943. Visitors often chatted with patients through open windows.

"The soldier left," said Mici, "but was back next day and insisted he had more orders 'to finish this neck of the woods.' So I called all the ladies to the danger, and we put chairs under the trees and sat on them. So what could he do?"

To celebrate the victory, a spontaneous tea party was held the next day beneath the shade of the pines.

Sometimes referred to as Shangri-La, Los Alamos was not a mountain paradise with all the conveniences. There were no telephones in homes, nor bottles of milk, nor rolled-up newspapers on doorsteps in the mornings.

Los Alamos was not a mountain paradise with all the conveniences. There were no telephones in homes, nor bottles of milk, nor rolled-up newspapers on doorsteps.

Electricity was uncertain, failing many times during the dinner hour when all the hot plates and electric roasting ovens in town were in use. These were preferred by the women over the wood-burning cooking stoves that had been converted to use kerosene and dubbed "Black Beauties," for they were "hideous, curvaceous and very black," wrote Wilson.

With people cloistered together in isolation on the restricted mountain top, it is not surprising that tensions mounted and tempers flared.

Laura Fermi (wife of Italian Nobel laureate Enrico Fermi) thought that the Army doctors had a thankless job. Doctors were prepared for the emergencies of the battlefields. Fermi wrote, "instead they were faced with a high-strung bunch of men, women and children ... high-strung because we were too many of a kind, too close to one another, too unavoidable even during relaxation hours, and we were all (as Groves had warned his officers) crackpots; high-strung because we felt powerless under strange circumstances, irked by minor annoyances that we blamed on the Army...."

ımanding officer acquiesced to the civilians' ed a Town Council to function as a link ıority and civilian autonomy. The Council did ve or policy-making clout. "It never made of ıe of convenience and gracious living, but as a eam it was a great success," commented e Smith.

the Council expanded ıbers, elected every six he commanding officer ;e of the Council and ı Army representative, the people why military simple request. He ‹ to the military ıe confounded civilians

ıncil received complaints dormitories. Usually, ier-husband based on rumor of one sex ·w a record crowd to packed wall-to-wall in dining room, were entertained by the antics of ising young star in physics (and a Nobel delighted in confounding the Army. ived in Los Alamos, he was determined to lormitory room to himself. His wife, ill with arby in Albuquerque, but he had a box of her t seem that there was someone else in the ıtgown on the bed, rumpled the bed, and he bathroom. He continued this prank for e danger that they would put a second person eynman explained what happened: cleans the rooms in the dormitory opens this lden there is trouble: Somebody is sleeping ! Shaking, she doesn't know what to do. She ıarwoman, the chief charwoman reports to ·utenant reports to the major. It goes all the generals to the governing board. What are

Single-family homes were little more than camping trailers; several dormitories housed single men and women.

ılgated a rule," wrote Feynman. "No Women ry!" That little ruse got him elected to the nting the dormitory faction.

The Pajarito Plateau sits above the Rio Grande on the east flank of the Jemez Mountains.

"There were always rumors," said Beckie Bradford (later Becky Diven), a dormitory representative to the Council. In Bradford's dorm, women ranged in age from 20 to 45 years. "We worked many shifts at odd hours. No wonder the rumor mill worked overtime," she said.

Meanwhile, the Council and Army command wrestled with other issues of mesa business such as traffic violations, rent raises, snapping dogs, inadequate restaurant facilities, appalling sanitary conditions in the trailer area, playgrounds for the children, transportation to Santa Fe, and maid service.

In spite of the annoyances when things went wrong, and generally there was never a day they didn't, Wilson wrote, "It was a Barnum and Bailey World .... We loved it."

Although Los Alamos was "plain, utilitarian and quite ugly," Brode observed that one could look beyond the steel fences and watch the seasons pass. She wrote, "The aspens turning gold in the fall against the dark green evergreens; blizzards piling up snow in winter; the pale green of spring buds; and the dry desert wind whistling through the pines in summer. It was a touch of genius to establish our strange town on the mesa top."

Many attributed that genius to Oppenheimer, whose love of physics and the desert country brought together people dedicated to the same mission. Six mornings a week, at 7 and 7:30, Oppie's whistle blew, calling the people to the grind. They walked or rode bicycles to work, seldom using a car to preserve precious gasoline rations.

Behind multiple strands of barbed wire fence, they disappeared into a secret world where they spent long and arduous hours, often sleeping on a cot if an experiment went late into the night. The tireless achievers knew they were engaged in an important wartime effort. Brode wrote, "Even an outsider like myself, with no idea what the problem was, could feel the inner urge for scientific solution." Brode even asked Segrè, "What on earth are we hatching here?"

Segrè replied, "What we do here, if we do it, will make a revolution, like electricity did."

Rest and Relaxation

Though an urgency to complete the scientific mission prevailed, the top brass in the military and civilian camps encouraged and supported recreation.

George T. Fike, then a corporal in the Army, was assigned to Los Alamos as the post recreational director. "As far as recreation was concerned, we had to cater to GIs, Wacs, and civilians alike," said Fike.

"We had just about every type of entertainment," he said. There was baseball, touch football, basketball, tennis courts that were part of the Ranch School, a nine-hole golf course with sand greens, horseback riding for 50 cents an hour, ice skating, skiing, movies, and plays.

"Theatre No. 2 saw a lot of action," said Fike. From early morning until late at night, it functioned as a gymnasium, movie house, dance hall, church, and auditorium. Beneath the building was a basement where Fike's office was located as well as lockers for the basketball players. The area was also used as a dressing room for the Little Theatre group who staged many plays there. Fike remembered that one special hit was *Arsenic and Old Lace*.

"The high spot of the show was the end of the last act when the dead bodies were brought up from the cellar," wrote Brode. "It was kept top secret so well that the audience was unprepared to see first Oppenheimer brought up stiff as a corpse and laid on the floor, then William (Deke) Parsons, then Bob Bacher, Cyril Smith, Harold Agnew, and others." The corpses, highly respected leaders of the scientific effort, delighted the audience. After the performance, the audience followed tradition, pushed back the chairs and benches and danced until midnight to music provided by the local jazz band.

Top: From early morning until late at night, Theater No. 2 functioned as a gymnasium, movie house, dance hall, church, auditorium, and so forth; middle: KRS radio broadcast daily from the Big House; bottom: party-time was synonymous with Saturday nights.

An appreciative audience enjoys the talent of pianist Ernie Titterton of the British Mission; toes tap to the spirited tunes of Willie Higinbotham playing his accordion, nicknamed "the Stomach Steinway."

On one such evening at the Segrès' home, guests sat quite still to hear Danish Nobel prize winner Niels Bohr tell of his experience outwitting the Germans when he escaped from Denmark to Sweden. Bohr spoke softly, his voice heavily accented and often interrupted by the constant lighting of his pipe.

"We even had a radio station, KRS," said Fike. The electronics equipment needed to build the station was appropriated from the Technical Area, and one of the scientists installed it. "The station was unique as it radiated from a telephone wire—that was the antenna," said Fike. "We had no license, but we had a radio station." The station had a narrow broadcast range that could not be heard off the Hill.

Often, people loaned their records to the local station to be played or they offered to perform for the small listening audience. Once a week, for 15 minutes, Al Bartlett read poems by Robert Service. Otto Frisch, a German physicist, played the piano. Fike and Bob Porton, who became a fixture at KRS and who later worked for the Public Affairs Department at the Laboratory, co-hosted a show called "Lunchtime with Tom and Bob."

Party time was synonymous with Saturday nights. Seldom was there not a party in full swing, either "big and brassy or small and cheerful."

Typically, dormitory parties were well attended. People stood elbow-to-elbow in the common rooms, emptied of all furniture for the occasion, except for the punch bowl. A huge, glass chemistry container, about 5 feet in diameter, was borrowed from a laboratory and filled to the brim with a brew of liquors, whatever the organizers could get in Santa Fe. Sparingly, a few small cans of fruit juice were added for color. In the center of the wicked punch floated a large chunk of ice donated by the PX. In spite of too much liquor, too many people, and too much noise, people behaved in a seemly fashion and adhered to the unwritten rule that "doors to rooms remain open." As Swiss physicist Hans Staub liked to observe from a comfortable chair, "Thees place ees too schmall for that kind of thing. Everyone can see if you meesbehave, so eet ees not posseeble, that's all there ees to it."

If dormitory parties were the biggest and brassiest, there were many small dinner parties with varied themes. One hostess preferred formality right down to the finger bowls while another dished up food straight from black cooking kettles. Conversation among the party goers was highly spirited and lively, but at times quieted to serious and tense talk.

On one such evening at the Segrès' home, guests sat quite still to hear Danish Nobel prize winner Niels Bohr tell of his experience outwitting the Germans when he escaped from Denmark to Sweden. Bohr spoke softly, his voice heavily accented and often interrupted

by the constant lighting of his pipe.

He and his wife, Margrethe, had huddled in the dark of a gardener's shed until night, when they were hustled across a barren beach into a motorboat that sped them to a fishing vessel. Under moonlight, the vessel maneuvered through German mine fields and skipped detection by German patrols, finally landing in Linhamm, Sweden. Their sons would follow them later, aided by friends. Bohr, targeted for assassination by the Nazis, was forced to flee Sweden, along with his physicist son, Aage, for England, where he was persuaded to join the British team. He and Aage then flew in an American bomber to the United States, where they remained until the end of the war. His wife stayed in Sweden with their other sons.

Officially, Bohr's pseudonym was Nicholas Baker, but on the Hill, the Dane was affectionately known as "Uncle Nick." He and Aage "were very famous physicists," wrote Feynman. "Even to the big shot guys, Bohr was a great god."

When consulting at Los Alamos, the Bohrs were frequent guests at the Saturday night parties that had become an "integral part of mesa life."

Not a seat to spare in this Army vehicle as everyone enjoys a Sunday outting; the area surrounding Los Alamos offers abundant recreational opportunities.

The parties were regular social events, "pipelines through which we let off steam," wrote Jean Bacher, but so were Sunday trips. Whether by car, on horseback, or afoot, people left the site for some part of the day, summer and winter, to explore the Pajarito Plateau, a vacation land quite literally theirs during the war.

On Sunday mornings, the whistle was silent, and it was considered unsporting to work extra hours on the one free day of the week. In fact, General Groves was so adamant that people "get off the mesa" once a week, he ordered the issuance of B gas coupons for excursions.

On Sunday mornings, the whistle was silent, and it was considered unsporting to work extra hours on the one free day of the week.

Those fortunate enough to own a vehicle had the opportunity to escape the mesa top and their neighbors, but instead they usually invited friends or singles from the dorms to fill the empty spaces and share the trip planned for the day. "Eight in the car was considered the minimum patriotic load," wrote Bacher.

There were picnics at the Valle Grande (part of the Valles Caldera, a collapsed volcanic field west of Los Alamos), replete with tablecloths, cocktails, hot food, coffee, and cigarettes. Sturdier souls stuffed sandwiches into their pockets and hiked to the tops of mountains such as Lake Peak, Redondo, Tschicoma, Caballo, and Pajarito.

Archaeological buffs ranged over the mesa tops in search of obsidian arrowheads, scattered potshards, and petroglyphs of plumed serpentine figures, deer, birds, or geometric designs

Avid skiers seldom passed up an opportunity to ski. Left to right are Carl Buckland, Walter Kauzman, Kay Bentzen, Perc King, Beckie Bradford, Jim Wood, Jim Coon, and Ozzie Swickard.

During that first winter, several heavy snowfalls covered the landscape with a country snow, fresh and white. Exuberant fans of winter sports took to the outdoors with zest, enjoying sledding, snowshoeing, ice skating, and skiing.

scratched or painted onto rock surfaces by prehistoric residents.

Mysteries of the Anasazi Indians drew people to Bandelier National Monument, where cave homes with blackened walls from ancient fires were carved into the tuff cliffs. With the lodge and museum closed during the war, a single ranger scheduled lectures and tours that were announced in the *Daily Bulletin* published by the Army.

The foreign visitors were less fascinated by the Indian ruins. Living Indians intrigued Enrico Fermi more than dead ones. Fermi also preferred to scale the nearby mountain peaks, a hobby shared by Hans Bethe, L.D.P. (Perc) King, Segrè, and many others.

Segrè was content to hunt for mushrooms in dark, damp places or reel in big trout from cool mountain streams. He told newcomers, "All you have to do is throw in a line and they bite you, even if you are shouting."

A small equestrian contingency, which included the Oppenheimers, received special permission to purchase horses from local ranchers and to stable them with the remuda kept by the Army for the purpose of patrolling the back country. On Sundays and sometimes after work, riders saddled their mounts and rode into the raw wilderness, breaking trail through forests of tall pines and quaking aspens.

Numerous tales circulated about lost saddles, thrown riders, and runaway horses, summarily rounded up by the Army.

An outing one day erupted into high adventure for a group of avid women riders. On a ridge above Los Alamos, they spotted a lone person with a spy glass aimed at a building below. With the fate of the country at stake, they chased the "enemy spy" to within gunshot range. Much to their astonishment, a member of the group drew a revolver that she always carried. She said, "My husband insists I load the first two shots with blanks, but from there on I can do some good." But before a shot was fired, the spy escaped. The patriots reported the incident to the military police, who searched the area, but the spy had vanished.

Not everyone enjoyed athletic endeavors; some preferred a quiet Sunday, reading or listening to their favorite classics. Brode wrote that strains of Bach, Beethovan, or Mozart often filled the air. Groups of musicians formed ensembles and met at someone's home to practice and share their appreciation of music.

Edward Teller's Steinway grand piano filled all the space in the living room of his Sundt apartment. Willie Higinbotham's accordian, dubbed the "Stomach Steinway," went to all the parties. His peppy rhythms and shouts were a favorite with the square dancers.

Skiers relax by the saddle near Pajarito Mountain. Shown left to right are the Friedlanders, Cliff Garder, Nora Rossi, Don Kerst, Freddie DeHoffman, and Bob Carter. Skiers enjoy a day off in the mountains.

During that first winter, several heavy snowfalls covered the landscape with a country snow, fresh and white. Exuberant fans of winter sports took to the outdoors with zest, enjoying sledding, snowshoeing, ice skating, and skiing.

A favorite spot that attracted large crowds was Douglas Pond, a skating arena located on the floor of Los Alamos Canyon. The pond was only marginally maintained by the Army, but people didn't mind skating on the rough ice.

Deke Parsons, at the urging of his wife, Martha, agreed to an evening of ice skating with friends. But the man who would later arm the 'Little Boy' atom bomb while in flight on the Enola Gay found himself paralyzed on skates and instead clung to a bench, immobilized to such an extent not even his young daughter Clare could get him to budge. "He would not take one inch of progress the entire evening," wrote Brode.

In November of 1943, an informal ski club was organized to sponsor winter activities, mainly ski trips into the wilderness. Most new skiers outfitted themselves with Army ski equipment: white army skis (7 feet long and purchased for $5), soft leather boots that strapped into bear-trap or cable bindings, bamboo poles with large baskets, and seal skins.

Referring to the seal skins, Beckie Diven said, "They were wet things we wrapped around our waists going downhill but climbed up with them on our skis. We mostly climbed when I first came. It helped you develop good strong legs."

Diven felt fortunate to be invited on many trips since only a few people had cars, which they hated to have shaken apart on terrible roads, plus she had no gasoline coupons to contribute to the trip.

In April of 1944, Diven was part of a group of eight who decided to attempt a three-day backpacking ski trip into the Pecos Wilderness. Organizers of the group, Robert Williams

Right: Aerial view of the Jemez Mountains, with Pajarito Mountain in the middle and Ashley Pond and the Ranch School buildings in the foreground. This photograph was taken before the Army built a technical area around the pond. The open meadow in the center is the location of the first permenant housing built in Los Alamos after the war—Western Area. Above: Early Los Alamos skiers hiked more than they skied.

and Walter Kauzman, had secured permission from Oppenheimer to take the trip, which began at Cowles, New Mexico. On their first day out, the group came to a beautiful slope that they just had to ski.

"Lots of us thought we were getting to be pretty good skiers," said Diven. "Jim Coon tried a telemark. It was a disaster, and he had a spiral break in his lower leg. All of our camping equipment was at least hours away from us. We knew from a map that the nearest place was a small shelter, Jarosa cabin. We made a toboggan from skis (the Army skis had holes drilled into their tips for this purpose). I was the only one who had ever splinted a leg before, so that became my job, to splint Jim's leg. We all contributed clothing to wrap him up, and it was very slow and arduous climbing to the cabin ... there was some oatmeal and dried apricots and since I was the only girl there they said, 'You cook.' I didn't even know how to cook, not oatmeal and apricots. We huddled around the fire and put sleeping bags around us as best we could. Meanwhile, two members of the group had skied 13 miles back to a ranch in Cowles to telephone for help because it was obvious we couldn't possibly get out."

Shirley Barnett, whose husband, Henry, was the pediatrician in Los Alamos, remembers the midnight call for help. The boys, she recalled, were told to wait at the ranch to direct the rescue party.

"Immediately, the doctors went into a huddle to plan the rescue," wrote Barnett. "They would need an ambulance, a toboggan, and a skiing doctor. They discovered the only skier among them was Henry, a weak skier at best who had already been up for two nights with a hospitalized child.

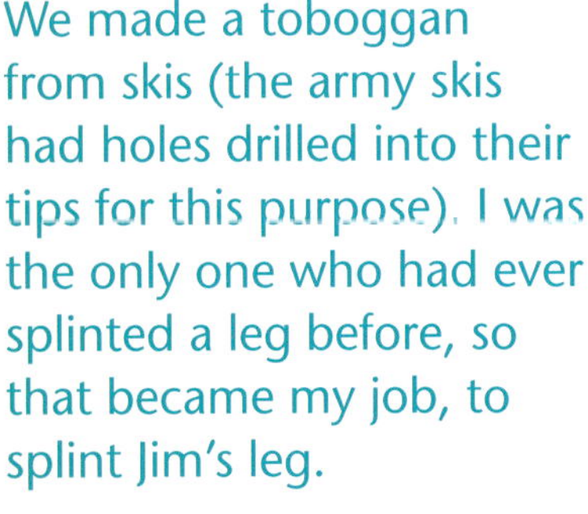

We made a toboggan from skis (the army skis had holes drilled into their tips for this purpose). I was the only one who had ever splinted a leg before, so that became my job, to splint Jim's leg.

"Even after rousing people all over the mesa, they failed to find a toboggan," wrote Barnett.

Someone remembered that there was a doctor at Bruns Hospital in Santa Fe who had trained Army troops in ski rescue techniques. Since he was obviously the man for the job, Shirley was relieved to think that perhaps Henry would not have to be the one on call this night, but the Bruns doctor had just had his upper teeth extracted that afternoon, so the burden of rescue fell back on Henry.

The assembled rescue team included an ambulance and a driver, medical supplies, food, and a toboggan. In addition, a young and able skier, Hugh Bradner, was aroused from his sleep to accompany Dr. Barnett and a surgeon, Dr. Jim Nolan, who would spell Barnett once the injured man was in the ambulance. The party departed on a cold Monday morning at 2 a.m.

Diven thought Dr. Barnett had been on skis maybe three times. "Poor Dr. Barnett got up there on his hands and knees, and we often thought at the time maybe he would have to come out on a toboggan. Upon arrival, the doctor administered morphine to Coon and splinted his broken leg. The next day the doctor revived and did very well."

Early Tuesday morning, the party began its descent, but the going was difficult with drifts of snow up to their thighs.

"Unable to make it back to transportation, we broke into a cabin ... on the shelves were rations; macaroni and cheese and other staples like that, so that was our dinner," said Diven, "a gooey mess because, again, I was the cook."

By noon on Wednesday, the rescue team reached the ranch, where Coon was transferred to the ambulance and transported to Bruns Hospital. He was diagnosed with two broken bones in his lower leg.

The incident caused feelings of alarm: the skiers had taken unnecessary chances and had placed the project and its employees at risk.

"The rest of us came back to considerable notoriety and great ire on the Hill," said Diven.

Shirley Barnett wrote, "Henry felt he would not survive another trip like that. He heartily encouraged the rest of the medical staff to take up skiing and helped form a committee to pass on all plans for hiking, hunting, and skiing trips."

"It was remarkable that Jarosa cabin was there" said Coon, "and it was fortunate I did not have a compound fracture." During the tedious trek out of the wilderness, Coon remembered feeling "fairly comfortable, and I kept thinking how lucky, really lucky I was." Coon's sense of humor sparkled in his eyes when he said, "My claim to fame is that I was the first laboratory person to break a leg skiing."

From top: Perc King surveys the slope before pushing off a cornice; a lone skier in a winter wonderland; Enrico Fermi (in brimmed hat) insisted on getting out each weekend to see nature, according to Perc King.

Part Two
Sawyer's Hill

The Rope Tow

It was a chilly day in February 1944 when the California Limited, enroute from Chicago to Los Angeles, rolled into Lamy, New Mexico. Except for the train depot, a restaurant, and a few humble homes, the small railroad town seemed forgotten in its desert solitude.

Aboard the train were several young students who had been mustered out of college, drafted into the Army's SED, and assigned to Los Alamos. Juggling duffle bags stuffed with a few belongings, the SEDs stepped into the bright sunshine and stretched their legs. Some smoked while others speculated about their mission. One veteran SED, Neil Davis, remembered that moment, "My gut feeling was I didn't have control of anything."

But John Rogers' attention was riveted on the rugged, snow-capped peaks of the Sangre de Cristos that loomed ominously on the horizon. As a youth, he had enjoyed ice skating and sledding down the rolling hills of his homeland at the confluence of the Missouri and Kansas rivers. Rogers said, "Immediately, I knew I was going to learn to ski." He had always wanted to ski and described the emerging sport as "fascinating in those days with the old black-and-white movies, a novelty."

The tiny town of Lamy, New Mexico, train depot for the Santa Fe Railroad, and the arrival point for most of the Manhattan Project personnel, has changed little since this photo was taken in the 1930s.

Although anxious to end a trip that had begun days before, the SEDs slowly boarded the drafty Army bus that would take them to McKibbin's office in Santa Fe before their journey to the up yonder.

When the bus stopped at the guard gate at the east entrance to Los Alamos, the military police issued the SEDs temporary passes. That was when Davis saw his first submachine gun.

Quarters for the SEDs were the Army barracks. Their barn-like interiors were stark and dim, as General Groves had ordered them to be built to offer only minimum comfort. The only comfort features were several potbellied stoves lined in a row along the center of the long building. "Their warmth helped make life comfortable," said Neil Davis. "At least bullets weren't flying at you."

At first, routine for the SEDs was extremely regimented, with early morning drills, bed inspection, and long work days. George Kistiakowsky wrote that the SEDs "really felt themselves the pariahs of Los Alamos."

Since the SEDs were not combat troops and since the scientists depended on the SEDs, Kistiakowsky tried to convince the Army brass to relax the discipline but wrote, "I got absolutely nowhere."

Eventually, the SEDs got a new commanding officer and, ultimately, drills and bed inspections were dropped to allow for extra sleep after long nights in the Tech Area shops.

Energetic and free-spirited, the SEDs did not need urging to heed General Groves's directive to take recreation on Sundays.

Rogers soon acquired, for $5, a pair of wood mountaineering skis, bear-trap bindings, and the last pair of soft ski boots and metal poles to be found in Santa Fe. The heavy skis, he said, "were ski trooper skis, big stiff boards made for big boys with 60-lb. packs on their backs."

In the beginning, skiing involved a lot of climbing. "I used Army mohair skins," said Rogers, "but mostly we used herringbone or side steps, things like that if we were going uphill. We had wonderful instructors—Fermi, Bethe, and those guys from the old country who skied the Nordic style, telemark. And we did this with 7-foot Army skis."

Rogers had the idea to build a rope tow, although he does not recall when, but it was an idea other skiers liked.

George Kistiakowsky had the interesting idea of cutting trees using plastic explosives.

In the summer of 1944, a few folks volunteered their Sundays to help widen the existing slope at Sawyer's Hill, just west of Los Alamos on the road to the Jemez Mountains. These slopes were originally cut by Herbert (Hup) Wallis, an instructor at the Ranch School. The plan was to clear trees for a new tow path higher up on the north edge of the slope.

"We were amateurs at felling trees," said Robert Williams, "and had some close calls with trees falling in unexpected directions."

George Kistiakowsky's specialty was explosives. He was an associate division leader at the Laboratory under Deke Parsons in the Ordnance Division. Often, he supplied explosives that were used to "cut" down the trees. "We'd build a half necklace around the tree, and the explosion cut it as if you had a chain saw," wrote Kisty.

Energetic and free-spirited, the SEDs did not need urging to heed General Groves's directive to take recreation on Sundays.

"Kisty thought prima cord wrapped around a sapling was very effective," said Williams, "but so was a hit with an ax."

As pressure to complete the war project intensified, progress at Sawyer's Hill slowed. It wasn't until October that Rogers persuaded a couple of working cohorts, Don Garrett and Bill Vogel, to share in his enterprise.

"They were outdoor types, and I guess anybody in Los Alamos had to be in order to survive," he said. "We all wanted to ski, so we set out to build the rope tow."

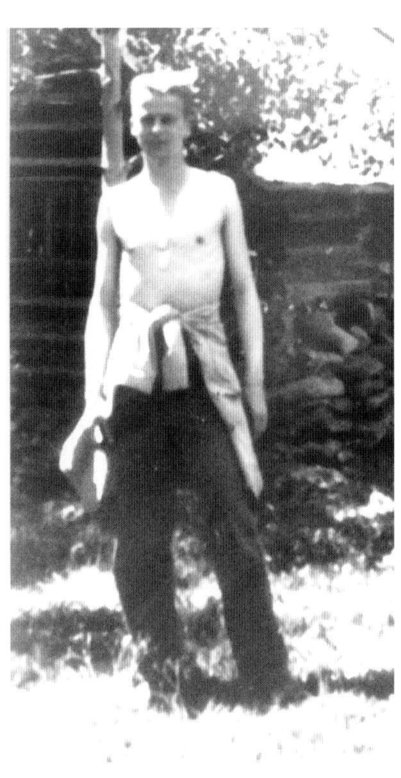

John Rogers, shown here at Camp May in 1944, played an instumental role in getting a ski area opened at Sawyer's Hill.

For parts they would need a motor, a rope, and pulleys for the tow. Thus, the three agreed on a business arrangement.

"I fronted out for all the expenses," said Rogers. "In my frugal youth, I had saved a few dollars. I was a wealthy person in those days because I was able to send home for a few hundred dollars."

But it was Garrett who owned the Ford Model-A roadster that he drove without its top on. It would get them to Albuquerque, where they planned to buy the tow parts.

"He was a different kind of entrepreneur," said Rogers. "Gasoline was scarce during the war and was illegal to burn without a coupon, yet kerosene could be purchased without one, so Garrett rigged his car with a five-gallon can filled with kerosene that he placed in the back of the trunk."

Rogers explained that when the gasoline expired, Garrett could circumvent the system by switching to kerosene. To accomplish this maneuver, he wound a copper line along the exhaust manifold to enhance vaporization so the kerosene could function more like gasoline.

One Saturday before dawn, the trio left for Albuquerque, a long and tedious trip, twisting over a narrow two-lane highway. Once in the city, they located a junk yard near the University of New Mexico that had a 1932 Chrysler engine and some Model A wheels that could be used for pulleys. They bought the lot for $35.

Satisfied with their purchases, though uncertain the engine would run, they began the long trip home. As they anticipated, the roadster ran out of fuel between Albuquerque and Santa Fe. Stranded on the shoulder of the highway, they waited for an hour before a vehicle passed them. The driver of a Cudahay meat truck came to their aid. He had a rope and said he could tow the disabled car into Santa Fe.

"What happened then," said Rogers, "scared me to death ... really frightened ... I was so stupid."

Speeding toward Santa Fe at 40 miles per hour, the roadster developed a flat on the left rear tire. Garrett, driving with a broken wrist immobilized in a cast, honked the horn repeatedly to alert the driver of the meat truck, but he didn't heed the blasts. In a desperate attempt to attract the driver's attention, Garrett constantly blinked the headlights and swerved the car back and forth. Still, the truck continued to speed down the dark highway. The situation was perilous! Something had to be done!

Rogers took action! With a knife in hand, he climbed over the windshield and stretched along the hood of the roadster. While the wind whipped at his clothes and forced his eyes to water, he managed to secure his footing on the front bumper. Bracing himself, he reached out to grasp the taut rope in his left hand and began to cut with his right.

"I suddenly realized that I am out on a limb because I had hold of the rope beyond where I was cutting," said Rogers. "It dawned on me the foolish nature of what I was doing. The separated rope would yank me off and I would have gone underneath the car and gotten killed. Panicky, I reached over to these two headlights that sat up on the bumper, grabbed a bar between them and got my confidence back. Very gingerly, I cut the rope."

Not until the roadster coasted safely to a stop did the truck driver notice the situation. After he assessed their dilemma, apparently he felt unable to be of further help and left them to change the tire. Ultimately, they hitched a ride to Santa Fe for gasoline, returned to the abandoned car, and finally arrived in Los Alamos to see the sun rise over the purple silhouette of the Sangre de Cristo mountains.

"That was the beginning of the first rope tow in Los Alamos," said Rogers.

Work on the tow began in the Laboratory's M-Building, where Rogers and Garrett assembled the drive mechanism for the tow.

"Los Alamos was really a wonderful place to work," said Rogers. "People helped you to do things, and we could use the project facilities to build things."

What kind of rope to buy became an issue for Rogers. He knew he could buy brand new sisal rope for the tow, but several scientists absolutely insisted on a particular rope fiber.

"The word came back," he said. "Gotta have manila rope."

The search for manila rope began in Los Angeles, California, where Vogel's father took charge of the project. He located remnants of the precious rope (referred to by Dave Inglis as "worth its weight in gold") from a defunct circus. Again, Rogers fronted the sum of $200 to buy the rope.

"Well, it was a white elephant," he said, "it was in very short lengths, 25 to 50 feet, as it was used to hold up tents. It was rotten, but it was manila rope."

But their efforts to install the tow were halted by Army regulations. The SEDs, being military, could not operate the tow as a business. Yet a private club could run the tow on the Post and could purchase the equipment from the owners, who in turn could then operate the tow for the club.

Bradner, Inglis, and Kistiakowsky interceded on behalf of the SEDs and proposed the formation of the Sawyer's Hill Ski Tow Association.

The three drafted a memo, dated November 3, 1944, that began with bold headlines: SKIERS! SKI TOW PROSPECTS WITH ENOUGH ENTHUSIASM, WE CAN HAVE A TOW AT SAWYER'S HILL—WILL YOU JOIN?

Prior to the memo, Inglis, Rogers, Vogel, and Garrett had provisionally agreed to certain conditions regarding liability, the tow's maintenance and operation, price of the equipment, and a payment plan by the club to purchase the equipment for $560. The fee to join the club was set at $7.50 for civilians and officers and $5 for enlisted

A sweeping vista from the Pajarito Plateau, looking toward the Rio Grande near Otowi Bridge.

"I suddenly realized that I am out on a limb because I had hold of the rope beyond where I was cutting," said Rogers. "It dawned on me the foolish nature of what I was doing."

personnel. If the club were to enter into an agreement with the tow owners, it would need a minimum of 80 people to join.

The memo further pleaded, "Please indicate your willingness to join. Don't wait to blame yourself for our not having a tow, or to regret the higher cost of membership later. Join now!"

Thanks to an early snowfall, plus the promise of a rope tow, people tuned their skis and responded heartily to the memo. By November 10, nearly 130 people had "pledged to contribute funds for the purchase and operation of the tow."

In the middle of the slope at Sawyer's Hill, mid-way up to the intermediate level, grew a large, stately Ponderosa pine tree called the Red Tree. "It was everyone's ambition to get to the Red Tree and come down," said Becky Diven.

However, a path for the tow had yet to be cleared through the woods, so volunteer work parties were organized to spend Sundays on Sawyer's Hill cutting timber. Also, a number of details between the Army, the ski club, and the tow owners had to be settled before any formal arrangements could be made.

Could they acquire non-highway gasoline to be used for the engine to run the ski tow? The War Price & Rationing Board 25 agreed to issue R-rations for this purpose.

Still, the interim committee knew they lacked authority and had limited resources for the rope tow, so they sought approval and support from the commanding officer, Colonel G.R. Tyler.

Although General Groves often fumed at the confusion that the civilian families brought to a military post, in his view, rest and relaxation for the residents of P.O. Box 1663* received top attention. So, the prompt reply by Tyler to support the association was not a surprise.

Tyler supported all seven issues raised by Kistiakowsky:

1. In principle, the organization of a nonprofit association to operate the ski tow on Government property is approved.

2. It is entirely satisfactory for military personnel of this command to participate in the activities of your association.

3. I have instructed the Post Engineer to comply with your request in regard to the inspection of the tow in order to pass on its safety; however, the results of this inspection will not in any way be guaranteed, but will merely be an opinion on the part of the Safety Engineer.

4. The Post Engineer has been directed to cooperate in keeping the four miles of road passable for passenger vehicles during the snow season. Moreover, he informs me that when there is a substantial snowfall during a short period of time, all available

---

**During the war, because of the secrecy of Los Alamos, all residents used this address in Santa Fe.*

personnel and equipment are busy for some time clearing snow from roads, streets and other areas which must be used for personnel in the pursuance of regular business. He further informs me that for this reason, it may not always be possible for him to keep the road passable for passenger vehicles. He will render such assistance as he can, but does not want to accept the responsibility of keeping it absolutely clear of snow. He states that at all times last winter, a passenger car could travel over the road by the use of chains.

5. The use of a Government vehicle for transportation of gasoline necessary for the operation of the tow is approved.

6. I am sure that arrangements can, under ordinary circumstances, be made for the transportation of skiers to Sawyer's Hill.

7. I have directed the Post Engineer to cooperate with your organization in the matter of sending a bulldozer to the hill for the purpose of clearing a larger parking and turning space for cars and buses. However, he advises me that in carrying out these directions at this time he would need to interrupt work which has been regularly authorized at this Post.Tyler concluded in his letter that his office would "render every possible cooperation since we are highly in favor of such recreation activities," but added a disclaimer, "the Government is in no way obligated or held responsible for construction, maintenance or safety measures."

Becky Bradford practices her snowplow turn.

At a meeting on November 13, the paid membership voted to accept a memorandum of agreement, a document that members had to sign which waived their rights and claims against the association. It was decided that minors, should they wish to ski, needed written authorization from their legal guardians or parents. They approved the agreement of sale between the sellers, Garrett and Vogel. Rogers had withdrawn his name from the original pact, wishing only to get his initial investment back. Members voted to amend the rules stating that a member could resign from the club but, in so doing, could not claim a refund on his dues. Lastly, they applauded David Dow for his contribution of drafting the various documents.

"Please indicate your willingness to join. Don't wait to blame yourself for our not having a tow, or to regret the higher cost of membership later. Join now!"

At 9:12 p.m., the Los Alamos Sawyer's Hill Ski Tow Association, formed to own and operate a ski tow for the benefit of its members, was official.

Rogers remembered the association as "a collection of interested people who anted up the money. I got my investment back, and the three of us agreed to make that tow run for one winter."

Eager to get the tow operative before snow came, volunteers increased their efforts to help the SEDs finish the job.

"Those 25- and 50-foot lengths of manila rope had to be spliced together," said Rogers. "Not good rope, but it was manila."

"Many people spent many hours learning how to splice that rope," said Diven.

To accommodate the rope, extra wheels, borrowed from the Project, were attached in trees; at the top of the tow, a small car wheel functioned as the bull wheel.

"There was a safety gate at the top," said Rogers, "so if a skier was in trouble, he could hit the wire, the engine would stop, and he didn't get pulled into the wheel."

The engine, also placed at the top of the tow, was mounted on a wooden frame with steel stakes driven into the ground to secure it. The engine drove a wooden drum, which was about one foot in diameter and was made of laminated hardwood. The manila rope was wrapped around the drive drum many times.

The tow was finished in time for the ski season to open the day before Christmas.

"It ran little more than 400 feet," said Rogers, "but it was a beginning."

Luther (Rick) Rickerson, who operated the beginner's rope tow on Sawyer's Hill, remembered the local season-pass holders even though they had a little card to identify them.

Jim Coon thought that the rope tow was "the most amazing thing."

Harry Snowden was hired to be the regular tow operator. His main responsibility was to keep the tow running and to purchase the gasoline.

"I hauled those containers to the top of the tow," said Snowden, "hard and awkward work."

He also drove an Army dual-axle 6 x 6 truck that was used to transport the gasoline and the skiers over a narrow, snow-packed road that curved along the edge of the canyon wall with a steep drop. There wasn't a guard rail, and chains were usually necessary. Some skiers remembered the road as hazardous and scary in the winter.

Additional operators were hired to assist Snowden, who had to stay at the top of the lift with the engine. They checked membership badges, spaced the riders of the tow about 30 feet apart, shoveled snow onto the tow path if necessary, and made sure minors did not ride the tow unless authorized. Snowden earned $5 a day. His assistants could receive the same salary or choose a free ski membership.

Since Snowden operated the controls of the engine at the top of the tow path, Diven said, "He could not see the skiers at the bottom, so when skiers were ready to go, they'd yell 'OK Harry' and he would start the tow." Not only on the ski hill but around town, the famous phrase, "OK Harry," stuck to Snowden.

The first ski season got off to a bumpy start. At a January meeting, the board and members grappled with complaints from skiers who were dissatisfied that the tow did not start at the bottom of the hill, which meant they had to climb several feet to reach the tow. They demanded that their membership dues be refunded. After a prolonged debate, the majority of members voted to deny refunds.

Then Vogel rose to speak. Responsible for the technical management of the tow, he said that he was having difficulty with the influx of suggestions about maintenance that came to him from various members. He suggested that a technical committee be formed so members did not approach him directly. A motion was so made and passed to appoint such a committee.

But rope tow troubles persisted for the association. A memo from Nick Metropolis, president, explained the problem:

"The pressing matter of adequate maintenance of the tow by the association is now with us, inasmuch as the 'party of the first part'—the previous owners—are putting the tow in our laps...unless we provide for more adequate maintenance, the tow cannot survive."

"That bull wheel was not a smart thing," said Rogers. As the rope passed through the small diameter of the wheel, it would shred and break. He spliced rope two or three times a day when the tow operated.

Michael Poole, a member of the British Mission and a charter member of the tow association, recalled the homemade ski-lift at Sawyer's Hill. "The lift was made from a derelict engine and a lot of rope of doubtful antecedents." When the rope broke, it would "initiate a line of people skiing down the hill backwards," he wrote.

"I felt badly about that rope," said Rogers. "It was dirty, rotten, wet, and we didn't know much about splicing either.... We did short splicing and used lots of friction tape donated by the Project."

Snowden said, "Rogers was the 'stud buzzard' for keeping things going."

George Moulton, ski club president 1951–1952, displays his stem christy technique on Sawyer's Hill.

The New Sport—Skiing

In 1943, skiing was a novelty sport in New Mexico. People discovered the same thrill that the early gold miners in the mid-1800s had enjoyed. Norwegian skis were used not only for transportation across snow fields but also for the exhilarating sensation they provided when sliding down a snow-covered hill.

"People were frantically trying to learn to ski. They had not been exposed to skiing. They were here, with snow all around them," said Becky Diven. "It seemed like heaven to have it right here in town and not have to drive hours and hours."

Perc King had never skied when he arrived at Los Alamos from Purdue University in 1943, but he quickly became an avid fan of the sport after his friend, Don Kerst, took him to the Valle Grande for an afternoon of skiing.

"I did a little coasting on shaky legs," he said, "but after that introduction to skiing and having fun, I decided it was for me."

King said that it was Enrico Fermi who insisted on getting out every weekend to see nature.

Laura Fermi wrote that Enrico was "...bored by the monotony of going up and down the same incline," so he "formed a group who tackled more energetic cross country excursions and off they went."

"We had a nucleus of ski enthusiasts," said King, "and thanks to Fermi, he really got us skiing."

King remembered Fermi as "a good cross country skier who could coast down, a great outdoorsman."

After Enrico returned home from one of these trips, Laura recalled that he was happy and proud if he could tell her he had "out-tired much younger men than himself."

Many ski trips were taken by different groups to such places as Rabbit Mountain, Redondo Peak, Horses Head (below Santa Fe Baldy), Lake Peak, Pajarito Mountain, or Mount Inglis (unofficially named by the skiers for Dave Inglis, a skiing buddy who always liked skiing that particular mountain). King said that the ski trips required strenuous hiking.

From top: an unidentified group on a trip through the snow; Cliff Garner, third ski club president, races down a slalom course at Sawyer's Hill.

Skiers also enjoyed being pulled up the mountain by one of Kistiakowsky's ski mobiles, which he had acquired from friends in Washington. "I got a couple of ski mobiles which weren't like the modern ski mobiles but more like jeeps or tracks," he wrote.

"This miniature white tank towed skiers from the bottom of the trail run back to the top many times on a Sunday," wrote Jean Bacher. She recalled that it finally met its match on a trip to Redondo Peak, the highest elevation in the Valles Caldera, where the "drifts of snow proved too much for the weasel." It bogged down, and the skiers had a "weary walk home."

King recalled that groups of skiers would often go quite a distance to ski. Often, the trip was "mostly a hike, but it was always worth it ...great to get out into the wilderness in snow and just walk," he said. "We were just so crazy to ski that we were always in search of a patch of snow."

Skiers on the Slopes

In spite of the tow's shortcomings, skiers of all ages crowded the slopes of Sawyer's Hill, located about four miles beyond the back gate that guarded the western perimeter of Los Alamos.

Jean Bacher recalled that whole families would appear at Sawyer's Hill for the day as babysitters were "eternally scarce and on Sundays were almost nonexistent, unless one lived on Bathtub Row and offered a tub as bait." Babies, bundled in the Indian fashion, were "set down in the snow and sunshine well out of collision's way while their parents skied."

Laura Fermi would only tackle the lower slope of Sawyer's Hill, while her husband "undertook greater feats, ventured on farther snow fields, and climbed steeper mountains."

Brode recalled, "There were always too many trees, too many children and inexpert sportsmen for good runs."

Though the Army had been persuaded to place a warming hutment at the bottom of the slopes, skiers preferred to eat outdoors. "We had fun in the snow, building big fires and having hot picnic lunches."

The Sawyer's Hill Ski Tow Association had discussed the possibility of ski lessons but had decided against the project. The only way beginning skiers could learn to ski was to watch the best skiers and attempt to mimic their style of skiing, and there were several adept skiers who displayed diverse skiing techniques.

From top: Dorothy Kerst, Freddie DeHoffman, Bob Carter, and Don Kerst pose in front of the closed-up lodge at Hyde Park; Enrico Fermi, famous for his knickers, could tire out men much younger than he.

Perc King said, "Bob Walker was the skier to watch if one wished to emulate a good stem turn."

"King had a physicist's approach to skiing," said Robert Williams, "he advocated crouching as low as possible, almost touching his rear to the ground."

One of the few accomplished skiers was George Kistiakowsky, who demonstrated the popular European style of skiing.

"Kisty skied with two skis glued close together," said Darragh Nagle.

But most agreed that Joan Hinton was the first and foremost skier. Nagle said, "She was scornful of Kisty's style, saying 'it was for practice slopes.'"

According to Nagle, Hinton, a former member of the United States Olympic team, had a wide stance and just went from point A to B. "Her style was hellbent for leather," he said. "She usually came down the slope in one big swoop."

Joan Hinton, who had followed Fermi to Los Alamos, was the daughter of Carlotta Hinton, headmistress of a well-known progressive school in Putney, Vermont. She was also a descendant of Boole, the British mathematician of Boolean algebra fame, and a relative of

Courtesy and Safety Rules

The Tow Association had anticipated that there would be very heavy traffic on the slopes that winter, including a large percentage of novice skiers, so a list of courtesy and safety rules was issued to all members:

1. Fill in your BATHTUBS. When a skier takes a spill, he MUST climb back up to repair any damage to the slope. It's your fault if you spill, so why crab about fixing it up!
2. Don't walk on the slope of the trail without skis. If you see a non-skier walking up the trail, don't bash him on the head with your poles; just ask him politely to do his walking elsewhere.
3. No sleds, toboggans, or dogs on the slope or trail.
4. When you climb up the trail, look and listen for descending skiers. When descending, yodel (all right, then, yell) as you come to a turn.
5. Control makes a good skier—don't schuss down the hill without it. You may run someone down, and you're reasonably certain to break a ski sooner or later.
6. Try not to make your turn at exactly the same place everyone else does. This keeps the slope from developing ruts and bare spots, and besides it's good practice. When there is deep snow on the slope or trail, try to pack it evenly by side-stepping as you climb up, rather than letting it develop deep ruts.
7. Beginners, don't use the lower end of the trail for a practice slope. Someone coming down at high speed (which is what the trail is intended for) may have to choose between you and a tree.

Sir Geoffrey Taylor, the well-known British scientist who visited the lab a few times.

"She was a personality!" said Nagle.

Francoise Ulam described Hinton as "not only being very smart, she had the strength of ten men and had been very upset when she was prevented to go fight a fire in the Jemez Mountains because she was a woman." Ulam remembered that on one motoring trip to the Pecos, a tire went flat. "While three wise men (Otto Frisch, George Taylor, and Stan Ulam) stood around debating how to solve the problem, Joan rolled up her sleeves and changed the tire before their discussion was over. After the war, she went to live in China to participate in the Maoist Experience."

Genia Peierls, the Russian-born wife of Rudolf (member of the British Mission) who was described as being blessed with "a boundless enthusiasm for life and a fund of good sense," made her skiing debut at Sawyer's Hill.

Bob Williams said that he and Kistiakowsky were standing at the bottom of the hill when they saw Genia take a spill at the top. Flat on her back, she made no effort to stop. As she slid down the slope, she gained speed and skidded past the two of them into some low bushes and saplings that had not been cleared.

Williams said that Kistiakowski, knowing the nature of his countrymen, spoke out, "That is Russian fatalism!"

The undaunted Genia, who, according to a friend, "loved to tramp over the hills with about fifty pounds of groceries on her back," picked herself up and climbed the hill to the tow to try again. Records indicate she never joined the tow association.

Hans Bethe, who received the Nobel prize in 1967, said that he had skied with Peierls in Switzerland and though skiing downhill was not natural to her, he said, "she did the best she could and was a woman of absolute determination."

The day Niels Bohr came with friends to Sawyer's Hill and stood quietly at the bottom of the slope, Laura Fermi, charter member of the tow association, was there. She thought how nostalgic Bohr must have felt for the sport he had practiced in his youth. It was then that a young scientist loaned his skis to Uncle Nick. Fermi described the occasion:

"He gave himself to elegant curves, to expert snowplows, to dead stops at fast speeds and to stylish jumps that no one else on the slope could perform. He went on with no pause for rest, with no thought for the man who had taken his place (standing) at the bottom of the hill, ski-less. He quit only when the sun went down and darkness and a chill descended upon the snow."

Niels Bohr climbs to the rope tow at Sawyer's Hill. A serious skier, he had done a lot of skiing in Europe. This photograph of "Nicholas Baker," the code name for Niels Bohr, was a conspiracy by three different people who happened to have a camera on Sawyer's Hill that day. They wish to remain anonymous because photographs of this great scientist were strictly forbidden at that time.

When the spring sun ended the ski season, even the hardiest of skiers were glad for the warmth and an end to the smell of coal fumes from houses heated by the black fuel. Although the tow "was not particularly safe or satisfactory," said Williams, "it lasted the winter." The ski season had been a huge success, and plans to improve the tow and conditions at Sawyer's Hill were already in the works.

The Dawn at Trinity

In early spring of 1945, an aura of urgency and tension began to build in the Tech Area and around the town. Curiosity grew as key security people, along with a large force of the mounted military police, disappeared from the mesa. The grapevine buzzed with the word *Trinity*.

"Every woman had a different idea of what transpired in the Tech Area," wrote Eleanor Jette in her book, *Inside Box 1663*. She and Martha Parsons had speculated about the mission and noted that it did not require much detective work for them "to realize that the gadget was a bomb." When Jette's husband, Eric, departed for Trinity on the evening of July 15, his last words were, "If you stay up all night you might see something."

People gathered into groups and chose a vantage point from which to wait, to wonder, to worry, and to watch for the impending test that, if successful, could end the war in the Pacific.

"Then it came. The blinding light like no other light one had ever seen. The trees, illuminated, leaping out as one. The mountains flashing into life.... The atomic bomb has been born."

Some people watched from their porches while others slept, unaware of the impending event. One group drove south to the Sandia Mountains and camped for the night. Others huddled in the cold, gray dawn at the top of Sawyer's Hill, fearful for their husbands who had been off in the desert for endless weeks. What they couldn't hear were the conversations of the pilots in the observation planes talking to the ground, expressing fear that lightning from heavy thunderstorms might strike the tower that cradled the device. They didn't know that only one plane (piloted by Paul Tibbetts with Deke Parsons onboard) stayed to observe.

At 5:30 in the morning on July 16, 1945, in the bleak and barren land of Jornada del Muerto (Journey of Death), the device was detonated.

One of the wives, camped at Sawyer's Hill, wrote, "Then it came. The blinding light like no other light one had ever seen. The trees, illuminated, leaping out as one. The mountains flashing into life. Later, the long, slow rumble ... something wonderful ... something terrible.... The women waiting there in the cold are a part of it.... The atomic bomb has been born."

Jette described the moment, "Anxious eyes beheld a sunrise in the south. The sun rose and rose before it disappeared. The work was successful." At 10 a.m., one wife broke out a treasured bottle of whiskey, and the women raised their glasses to toast the men and women of the Manhattan Project.

Upon the men's return home, Laura Fermi wrote, "They looked dried out, shrunken. They had baked in the roasting heat of the southern desert and they were dead tired. Enrico was so sleepy he went right to bed without a word. On the following morning all he had to say to the family was that for the first time in his life on coming back from Trinity he had felt it was not safe for him to drive. I heard no more about Trinity."

Oppenheimer would later report, "Almost everyone knew that this job, if it were achieved, would be part of history. This sense of excitement, of devotion and of patriotism in the end prevailed."

After the atomic bombs were dropped on Hiroshima and Nagasaki, the Japanese at last surrendered. The war had ended. Work at Los Alamos slowed to an idle.

The Great Exodus, as it was called, began in earnest. Cars and trailers streamed down the main hill road.

With the initial mission of the Laboratory completed, uncertainties about the future of the Laboratory rippled through the town—should the Laboratory be abandoned? Those who bore intense regret and an anguished conscience over the bomb believed it should be devoted to research, basic and peaceful.

The future use and control of atomic energy was in question and lacked a national policy, leaving the Laboratory without a plan of operation for its future. Also, there was no guarantee that the University of California would continue to operate the Laboratory, as it had accepted the Los Alamos contract only as a patriotic gesture. Besides, many people had accepted their role in the mission as temporary and were anxious to leave behind the inconveniences of life on the Hill.

Many of the scientists prepared to return to lecture podiums and research programs at universities. The craftsmen and machinists looked for new, industrial jobs offering higher salaries. As for the SEDs, they eagerly waited to exchange their spartan life in the barracks for college dorms, academics, or other work.

Before the members of the British Mission departed, they invited their Los Alamos friends to a big party held at Fuller Lodge. On a September evening, guests wore their finest clothes and were announced as they passed through the formal receiving line. The guests enjoyed cocktails before the dinner that was cooked and served by the women and men of the British Mission. There was a thick soup, steak and kidney pie, trifles for dessert, and a variety of wines for the formal toasts, with the finest port, usually reserved for the King, the President, and the Grand Alliance. The Brits then staged an original pantomime that spoofed their arrival in the southwest, which they called the Unknown Desert.

Above: An appreciative audience enjoys the light-hearted entertainment in Fuller Lodge. This party, given before the British Mission departed, was the grandest party of all. It was an upper-crust event—people wore their finest clothing and were announced as they passed through a formal receiving line. Below: Members of the British Mission perform a skit that pokes fun at Security.

Philip Moon, member of the British Mission, recalled, "The thread of the pantomime was a frightened Britisher (Philip Moon) relentlessly pursued by Security (Jim Tuck dressed as the devil with a long tail that had attached to its end a real tail-light) and the Good Fairy, Winifred Moon, the only British wife who could display long pigtails with ribbon bows who came to the rescue."

The grand finale was a re-enactment of the Trinity test. Moon believed Tuck checked the text with Security as that would have been only prudent. "We had a number of words that might have been queried," he wrote. "Imaginary elements included dyspepsium and silentium, which was 'accidentally' dropped during the loading of the 'tower' and produced a loud bang."

Brode wrote, "the flashes and bangs and clatters for several minutes was not entirely comprehensible to many of the women, but made a tremendous hit with the men. It was a smash hit!"

At the end of the evening, a delightful, commanding colonel told Moon he would "never again allow it to be said that the British had no sense of humor."

Dancing followed the skit. The party was "one of the finer moments of the Grand Alliance," Brode wrote.

Among the British, several were charter members of the Los Alamos Ski Tow Assocation: Jim and Elsie Tuck, Bill Penney (later Sir William), Michael Poole, Greg Marley, and Klaus Fuchs.

A few days before the big party, Fuchs had driven his Buick to Santa Fe to purchase liquor for the event and to surreptitiously pass atomic secrets to a man named Harry Gold, an agent for the Soviets.

"Fuchs was a cipher to me; a faceless nonentity despite all the occasions we were in his company," Jette recalled. "When the light of day was turned on his treachery, I realized he was perfect in his role."

No one seemed to remember his skiing!

Partygoers enjoy a gathering at Fuller Lodge.

By the end of October 1945, most members of the British Mission had departed, along with hundreds of other scientists, technicians, and administrative personnel. The Laboratory staff had dipped from its wartime high of 3,000 to a mere 1,000.

For the first time in four years, the Peierls would be reunited with their two children, who had been sent to Canada for safety. Genia told a friend that when the blitz came to England, "What chance had my kids if the Nazis invaded ... my poor Jewish children with their Russian mother!"

The Fermis and the Brodes departed for home just before the New Year arrived. Oppenheimer had returned to peacetime duties and had appointed Norris Bradbury temporary director of one of the best-equipped research laboratories in the world.

Bradbury faced the confusion about him with a clear vision of the future. He believed research into military applications of nuclear energy would continue and that eventually the government would agree with him. He told his key staff members in an October 1945 meeting, "We should set up the most nearly ideal project to study the use of nuclear energy.... We have an obligation to the nation never to permit it to be in a position of saying it has something that it has not. The project cannot neglect the stockpiling and development of atomic weapons during this period."

The newly appointed head of the CM Division, Eric Jette, told his wife, "We've got to keep this place staffed and running until Congress decides what to do with it."

Bradbury would later recall, "In the months following the war the Laboratory struggled for existence, and there is no better way to put it."

Tow and Town in Transition

In the fall of 1945, after the World Series ended in a seven-game finish with the Detroit Tigers beating the Chicago Cubs, bets were made on the date of the first snow. While eyes looked to the sky for snow, the ski club focused on Sawyer's Hill and the improvement of the new tow.

Although the population had dwindled, the tow association expected ski attendance to exceed that of last season because great numbers of the military personnel had indicated an interest in skiing. Again, the commanding officer agreed to assist the organization.

"In spite of the fact that there is still a lot of work to be done on the new tow," read a memo to the membership, "with luck and lots of volunteer help, it should be ready to run by Christmas."

Most of the machining on the mechanical parts, designed by Bob Reedi, had been completed in the Laboratory's C-Shop.

"Things just seemed to appear," said Rogers, "like the four-cylinder International Harvester engine that showed up at Sawyer's Hill." And 2,000 feet of new sisal rope, one inch in diameter, replaced the rotten manila rope that had caused Rogers so much grief, but the new tow trail, set to the north of the old path, had some bumps that could cause serious wear on the rope. There was some discussion about adding two auxiliary pulley stations, but it was decided to keep only the lower pulley station and deviate the tow at that point. Roger Warner consented to design an adequate pulley system. He also suggested that the motor be placed at the base. Two hundred feet of new trail would have to be cleared.

The first bridge across the Rio Grande a few miles east of Los Alamos was a one-lane bridge near the tearoom of Edith Warner at Otowi.

Once more, Kistiakowsky suggested that dynamite be used to blow up the trees, in spite of a harrowing near accident that took place that summer.

Les Seely recalled that he and Kisty had spent a day on Sawyer's Hill, blowing up trees. Late in the afternoon, they had TNT left over, so they placed the explosives under a troublesome tree stump, about six feet in diameter. It blew up big, right over the treetops and onto Route 4, gouging a sizeable crater in the road. Seely said, "We looked at each other, turned white, and went home."

By November 8, 1945, it seemed iffy that the tow would be completed before the first snowfall. The pulleys were still in the shop. Volunteer workers were in a race with the weather to get the concrete foundation for the engine poured before it snowed.

"The ski tow was getting better and better on paper," wrote Bradford, who feared "it was going to stay on paper too long, as the designers had so much free time to think of improvements."

Hard work, youthful energy, and determined will combined to get the job done by Christmas. The SEDs installed the huge I-beams, the large pulley, and the new motor that they hauled to Sawyer's Hill in trucks. All eyes turned to the sky, looking for snow clouds.

The skiers prayed for snow, while the nonskiers prayed for no snow. "Those heavenly positions," wrote Diven, "seemed to be in conflict."

Lack of snow kept the ski hill closed and, worse, threatened the water system. Inadequate from the beginning, the main water pipes had not been buried deeply in the earth, as they should have been, but lay exposed on top of the ground. During the first two winters, plentiful snow covered the pipes and protected them from freezing, but a dry, bitter-cold December threatened to freeze the pipes. To compound the problem, the water supply slowed to a trickle due to the demands of an instant town on the mesa. Concerned about the water supply, the Army posted serious notices in the *Daily Bulletin*:

The TA-1 tech area, a tangle of buildings located along Trinity Drive and around Ashley Pond, functioned as Laboratory facilities until 1961.

October: "It would be advisable to limit the number of baths in each household to a minimum."

November: "After bathing the baby in the deep sink, save the water for the family wash. Please use dishpans for washing dishes. It is recommended that floors be scrubbed with water previously used for washing vegetables."

Brode wrote, "We took the position that if we were short of water it was up to the Army to get some more of it and stop fussing."

At certain times of the day, the water faucets would go dry, as authorities turned off the water when the level in the water tower was low. Then, two events happened almost concurrently. As the water situation worsened, the water reserves weren't replenished, and the taps were permanently turned off.

"The Major turned purple with rage and snapped, 'Madam, over my dead body will those pipes freeze up again,' and he stalked out of the hall."

Brode observed, "My faucets were the last to fail for we were in the lowest area, 'snob hollow' some called it."

Just one week before Christmas, the town learned that the main water line to the community had frozen solid. If there were a fire, the only water available to the firefighters was in Ashley Pond.

To supply water to the community, huge Army tank trucks hauled water from the Rio Grande. Daily, citizens gathered at the water tower where the water was dispensed as potable and non-potable, separate and distinct, clear or brown with heavy sediment. "Upon at least two occasions, I found Vermillion worms swimming in my treasured supply," wrote Jane Wilson.

"Parties were cancelled ... diapers went unwashed. The rudest thing one could do was use the bathroom in another house. The town plunged into a grim and grey period of mourning," wrote Wilson.

Bulletin notices ordered residents to boil all drinking water and "come to the hospital for typhoid booster shots at once, and flush toilets at least once a day for safety."

During the holidays, some families vacationed elsewhere so they could shower and escape the disaster. Jay Wechsler, a SED, said he followed the Army's suggestion to "take a water shortage furlough."

"Morale dropped to zero," wrote Brode.

At a Town Council meeting, an Army major faced an angry, chilly crowd waiting for an explanation on the disaster. He assured the skeptics that the pipes were being thawed and there would be running water as soon as the reserves were built-up. But one young housewife, in pigtails, wanted assurance that the pipes would not freeze again.

Brode wrote, "The Major turned purple with rage and snapped, 'Madam, over my dead body will those pipes freeze up again,' and he stalked out of the hall."

It would be several weeks before the pipes thawed. The town would wait until June before complete water service was restored. Thus, the only water available to many families continued to come from the Rio Grande.

Finally, snow fell in abundance, but it was short lived, so the ski season ended with only a fair rating.

In late spring, a few members explored the Camp May area and Pajarito Mountain (where they had previously skied) to search for a better ski area. However, most members, whose only experience of skiing was at Sawyer's Hill, lacked enthusiasm to move the tow, cut slopes, and argue for a road to be built to Camp May.

According to most members, the local ski hill (Sawyer's Hill) was better than anything else in the surrounding area.

In 1946, the Los Alamos Sawyer's Hill Ski Tow Association was retired and the Los Alamos Ski Club, a non-profit organization, was

Advice for beginners in a spring 1948 ski club memo read:

Bend your knees forward from the ankles at all times. This is part of the general effort to get your weight forward and to relax. Keep your knees bent when you walk, climb, run downhill, stem or just stand. In other words, bend your knees. From the safety point of view, it is hard to break your leg when it is bent at the knee—just try it!.

Don't ski too slowly. It may seem surprising, but all recent accidents at the Hill involved people standing still or moving very slowly. When first learning, pick a free line of run on a gentle slope with a good run-out (so you won't have trouble stopping) and then run it as fast as you can. This is not to be taken as encouragement for speed-crazy intermediate skiers.

Gain stability before attempting difficult maneuvers. Practice lifting one foot off the snow, jumping both feet off the snow, pumping up and down with your knees, running uphill, etc.

Buy a book on the Arlberg technique and bring it up to the slope with you for some hard work on the first few chapters.

Edith Warner: "A Bridge Between Two Worlds"

At a bend in the Rio Grande, near Otowi Bridge, a place the Indians called Po-sah-con-gay, "the place where-the-river-makes-a-noise," stood a small adobe structure. Here lived Edith Warner and her friend Tilano, a San Ildefonso Indian. Miss. Warner had arrived at this place in 1928 when A.J. Connell of the Ranch School had given her the job of overseeing the freight at a small boxcar railway station beside the bridge. To supplement a small income, Edith opened a tearoom.

It was on a dry and thirsty summer day in 1937, when a tall, lean young man dressed in blue jeans, boots, and spurs first stepped into the tiny, sparsely furnished tearoom. In her deerskin moccasins, Edith quietly served J. Robert Oppenheimer tea and "a slice of her magical chocolate cake," wrote Peggy Pond Church, daughter of Ashley Pond, in her book, *The House at Otowi Bridge*. In 1941, Oppenheimer would bring his wife to meet her. And Edith liked something about him. "His senses were alert as some creature of the woods. He had a poet's face, with eyes as blue as gentians and a mouth that was at the same time firm and a little wistful," wrote Church.

Edith and Tilano outside their home.

It was Oppenheimer who sensed the need for a brief respite from daily decisions, often agonizing, often made minute to minute, over the techniques of destruction being developed and to give the Lab workers, uprooted from their homes and cloistered in secrecy, a place to retreat and nourish their human spirit. Small groups of men and women filled Edith's house every night to dine. The meals were simple: herb flavored stew, posole, lettuce, sweet tomato relish, watermelon pickles, fresh bread, spiced peaches or apricots, dessert and steaming coffee. Reservations were made weeks ahead. About her home Edith wrote, "It was a house that stood for many years beside a bridge between two worlds." In her third Christmas letter, she wrote about that time:

"New Year's day of this historic 1945 held no hint of the atomic era. There were no blasts from the Pajarito Plateau making discord in the song of the chorus as I sat in the sun on an old portal at San Ildefonso."

"The climax came on that August day when the report of the atomic bomb flashed around the world. It seemed fitting that it was Kitty Oppenheimer who, coming for vegetables, brought the news. I had not known what was being done up there, though in the beginning I had suspected atomic research. Much was now explained. Now I can tell you that Conant and Compton came in through the kitchen door to eat ragout and chocolate cake; that Fermi, Allison, Teller, Parsons came many times; that Oppenheimer was the man I knew in pre-war years and who made it possible for the Hill people to come down; that Hungarians, Swiss, Germans, Italians, Austrians, French, and English have been serious and gay around the candlelit table. It has been an incredible experience for a woman who chose to live in a supposedly isolated spot. In no other place could I have had the privilege of knowing Niels Bohr, who is not only a great scientist but a great man. In no other way could I have seen develop a group feeling of responsibility for presenting the facts to the people and urging the only wise course—international control of atomic energy and the bombs.

"Perhaps the desperate state of the world and the anguish of millions as the constant backdrop of life intensified the joys that fall always brings. This year there were trips to the Plateau for wood on days when sky and aspen vied with each other in beauty. The wind made melody in tall pines while I gathered pine knots, those multi-shaped legacies of long forgotten trees. They seemed to be the essence of the elements garnered by a tree and now released in the fireplace to complete the cycle. Their gathering has become as much a part of the fall ceremonies as the garden harvesting and the southward flight of the wild geese. This rhythmic order of nature holds for me assurance as well as beauty."

Even scientists helped construct Edith's new home; Phil Morrison cuts a piece of Edith's magical chocolate cake for young Nick King, son of Perc King.

formed. Its sole purpose was to foster skiing at Los Alamos, to own ski tows and other equipment used commonly by its members, and to develop the facilities at Sawyer's Hill.

In order for the club to incorporate in the state of New Mexico, there had to be a provision for the division of assets of the club should it dissolve. If at any time the majority of members voted to dispose of the ski tow and club accessories, the excess cash from the sale of the equipment, after outstanding obligations were met, would be turned over to the New Mexico State Welfare Department to be used only for maternity and infant care in Rio Arriba County.

Housing is built in north community.

With Les Seely at the helm, the club made big plans to eventually extend the present tow and to install a beginner's tow on the lower slope. Fred Bemis and Bill Stein said they would give lessons to the neophyte skiers, charging civilian members $1 for an hour's lesson, GIs 50 cents, and nonmembers $1.25.

Concern for safety persisted. Plans were initiated to join the National Ski Association and form a ski patrol as part of the National Ski Patrol. Five people were recruited as ski patrol participants.

Other issues to face the club were budget, compensation for the volunteers, and conservation. Perc King said the balance in the treasury was only $358.73. Most members thought the balance too low and indicated there should be an increase of dues to "pump up the budget." But no motion was made to do so. However, a motion was made to give working volunteers a reduction in membership dues. It fell to defeat.

The ski club was cautioned by the United States Forest Service to "exercise a conservative approach in cutting down the trees." Apparently, sun on the slopes, which would melt the snow, was cause for concern. And, to prevent erosion of the slope, the project personnel agreed to plant grass and to limit the use of the bulldozer to avoid damage to the slope and trees.

Security had eased. At last, people could take pictures of their homes, the scenery, and their friends and send them through the mail.

In 1946, two years after the formation of the tow association, the ski club organization had matured from infancy to puberty. For Los Alamos, a blueprint of change was being drafted in Washington, D.C., and on the Hill. Good news cheered Los Alamos residents when General Groves approved plans for construction of the Hill's first permanent housing.

Security had eased. At last, people could take pictures of their homes, the scenery, and their friends and send them through the mail. However, pictures of the Technical Area, project public utilities, or security were still restricted.

The *Daily Bulletin* announced that free medical and dental service for civilians would end in July 1946. The bulletin also requested that all crutches and canes be returned to the hospital.

According to a May census, as reported in the *Los Alamos Times*, the drop in population steadied at 6,524 people. Sports preferences of the town included table tennis, badminton, swimming, bowling, dancing, golf, hunting, fishing, reading, and camping. Skiing failed to make the list, but softball and baseball dominated the summer scene. The Bombers, an SED squad in the Mountain Baseball League, were unbeaten, and the undefeated Wacs, who had won five consecutive softball games, would face an all-star team.

A hiker on the Pipeline Road poses with Pajarito Mountain in the background.

On the first of June, citizens were surprised by the Service Club's decision to slash the price of beer from 15 cents to 5 cents a bottle. Perhaps due to the water shortage, summer sales had soared, thus the Army had exceeded its permissible 5 percent profit.

The *Daily Bulletin* reported, "The GI's and civilians had high praise for the move." At last, the Army had done something right!

However, June 7, 1946, was a dark, somber day in Los Alamos. Residents were deeply saddened by the death of Louis Slotin, famed scientist and ski club member, who suffered from radiation exposure as a result of a Laboratory accident. Had Slotin not, with his bare hands, separated an assembly that had gone critical, many more deaths would have occurred. To honor his memory, a baseball field would bear his name. (This field was later changed into a neighborhood park known as Urban Park, and the baseball diamonds were moved to North Mesa, then known as Horse Mesa.)

The future of Los Alamos, as one of the key players in the nation's atomic energy program, seemed secured when Congress passed the McMahon bill, establishing the Atomic Energy Commission (AEC). Appointed by the President of the United States, the five-man civilian commission would have almost complete authority to oversee the domestic development of atomic energy.

General Groves sweetened the forecast when he announced plans to build a community center, replete with stores and services, at an estimated cost of $1,396,888.

Those pioneers—who had honored the call of their government to sacrifice the known for the unknown; who believed in their mission to rescue freedom from the oppression of Germany's Fuehrer, Adolf Hitler, and Japan's Emperor, Hirohito; who fell in love with their Shangri-La (Site Y, the Hill, the up yonder)—began to set down roots on top of the beautiful mesa that they hoped to call home.

News Bits

Excerpts from the *Los Alamos Times* documented the conversion of Los Alamos from a temporary community to one of permanence and the maturation of sports and recreational activities as the Manhattan Project gave way to the establishment of Los Alamos Scientific Laboratory.

March 7, 1947: Los Alamos Community Concert Association Present Trapp Family Program. A story book family come true are Baroness Marie Augusta von Trapp and her seven lovely daughters—the Trapp Family Singers.

March 7, 1947: Market Basket Column. Sally Taub reports that face soaps are returning to stock. Brown sugar is available...new is the jar of Armour Red Star pickled pigs feet at 30 cents.

May 2, 1947: Hill Worshippers Dedicate the Chapel. Los Alamos Chapel is a concrete symbol for the religious faith of the atomic workers where all hill denominations may worship.

May 2, 1947: Stables Open for Equestrians, Situated on North Mesa.

May 2, 1947: Tiano Brothers Who Own the Tiano Sporting Goods Store in Santa Fe will Occupy Building T 314.

May 2, 1947: Lights Underway for Night Games on the Softball Loop.

May 23,1947: The Project's Two New Supermarkets Open Their Doors on Monday Morning.

May 29, 1947: War Department Hands Over the Base Post Office to the Post Office Department.

The Big Snowfall of 1947

"It is snowing to beat the band, so I guess skiing is here for a while, along with the usual broken bones," wrote Beckie Diven. By December 12, 1947, Sawyer's Hill opened for ski business.

With its one-third of a mile of ski slope and two tows, 400 feet and 1,400 feet, Sawyer's Hill became a mecca for Los Alamos families. On one sunny Sunday, 225 skiers kept both tows operating full time.

However, just to reach Sawyer's Hill was a unique challenge. "You had a lot of handicaps," said Luther Rickerson.

There were two guard stations that one had to pass through. The first station was located at the end of the ice skating rink road on the top of South Mesa, while the second station was situated at the perimeter of Los Alamos County where the S-Site road intersects State Highway Loop 4. According to Rickerson, the guards would note the vehicle's license plate number and would allow it a reasonable length of time to pass between the two stations.

Another handicap was to remember to bring your pass. To forget was to commit a social faux pas! Once Joan Coon had hitched a ride to the West Gate with some bachelors, but had forgotten her pass. "It was a very quiet and grim ride back. I never forgot again."

May 29, 1947: Record Fish Catch of the Weekend was a German Brown Trout that Weighed 7 Pounds 4 Ounces and Measured 26 Inches.

July 3, 1947: Pastry Shop Concession Owned by George Hillhouse and Henry Martin will Open on Monday.

August 8, 1947: Water Shortage Threatens Said Zia Company due to an All Time Use of Water. Consumers were encouraged to curtail water use for thirty days. Failure to cooperate would be a serious hazard to fire protection.

August 8, 1947: Youth Center Gets New Facilities. Five New Booths, Ping Pong Tables, Soda Bar.

August 15, 1947: Council Seeks Services of Trained Town Planner. A recommendation that an experienced town planner be engaged to act as consultant with the community in organizing the government of Los Alamos, was made to the area manager in a joint report by the Town Council and the Community Association Council.

November 21, 1947: The First Female Wrestlers to Perform in Los Alamos Filled Theatre No. 2 to Capacity

November 21, 1947: First Snowfall of the Season on Monday Morning

November 14, 1947: Ski Club Motors to Wolf Creek Pass. Thirty Ski Club members plan to motor to Wolf Creek pass, Colo. Fortified with sleeping bags, food and ski equipment, they will camp in a U.S. Forest Service cabin whose only facilities are a large fireplace and running water.

Diven said that singles in the dorms developed a saying when everyone was packed into the car. "Boots-pass-poles-skis! Boots-pass-poles-skis!"

"If you lost the pass while you were skiing," said Rickerson, "you couldn't get back into town."

Once through the back guard gate, cars crawled up four miles of a narrow, twisting gravel road that had no guard rails. "It was unpaved completely," said Rickerson. "We didn't have graders in those days so we broke the trail. I used a 1947 Kaiser. I've seen it shovel snow up to the radiator. Of course I got stuck lots of times too."

At the urging of Bill Stein, Rickerson had accepted the job of operating the two rope tows plus selling daily tickets, which cost $1. "I usually left the house at six in the morning to get the tow going by 9:30," said Rickerson. "I'd load the car with some oil, electrical tape to wrap the splices in the rope and 20 gallons of gasoline stored in cans, which didn't keep my car smelling too well."

A former lift operator, Glen Waterbury recalled that the tows had to be handcranked, a tedious ordeal that could take 30 minutes. But Rickerson said the main tow was no trouble. "I had a five-gallon bucket of sand, and I would pour some kerosene in it, set the sand on fire, and set it under the motor. This warmed up the oil. Then you could crank it." But the beginner's tow didn't have a shed over it, so he had to wait for three or four fellows to come up on an icy morning to help pull on the rope to get the tow started.

"It was a day's work practically, trying to get that thing started on a cold day," said John Orndoff, who helped rebuild the drive on the beginner's tow. "You could almost tell who had cranked it that morning because the crank tended to fly off and catch you in the head."

"Once Les Seely got caught in the beginner's rope," said Orndoff. "We didn't have all the safety features we had later. Some of us nearby just grabbed the rope and held it until he got untangled."

Johnny Miller, a mock victim, is towed during a ski patrol toboggan practice.

Safety for skiers became a major focus for the ski club.

The *Los Alamos Times* reported: "While the ski club considers Sawyer's Hill to be one of the safest slopes for beginners, the safety committee, consisting of Leslie B. Seely, Jr., Dr. Jack E. Brooks, A.B. Conard and James Coon, is surveying conditions and studying past accidents on the slope with a view to increasing safety measures and educating beginners."

Steps were taken to level the approach to the little tow, additional safety signs were posted, the safety end gates on the tow path were improved, and a set of safety rules was distributed to ski club members.

Novices, unfamiliar with the hazards of skiing or of the slope, were reminded that ski patrol members, identifiable by their red arm bands, were available at all times for advice and assistance.

In January, winter struck with a bone-chilling fury. The mercury dropped to seven degrees below zero. Workers battled during the night to handle the cold wave emergency that crippled Albuquerque, Santa Fe, and Los Alamos. The *Los Alamos Times* reported that in spite of the Southern Union Gas Company's desperate effort to ration gas in all three communities it serviced, "the heat went out in all the homes.... People who didn't have fireplaces to burn just went to bed."

In early February, winter struck again, dumping 13 inches of fresh powder on the town, bringing the total snowfall of the season to 50 inches. Skiers were jubilant! The highlight of the season at Sawyer's Hill—Skiesta—took place on February 29, 1948.

The First Skiesta

On March 5, 1948, the *Los Alamos Times* reported:

"Witnessed by a crowd estimated at 300, the Los Alamos Ski club's colorful first 'skiesta' made a fair bid to become an annual crown to the winter sports season on the Hill. The steady stream of regulars and visitors had to plow through the churned-up road to Sawyer's Hill but the entertainment provided by the 2-1/2-hour spectacle soon dissipated the grumbles of drivers.

"Ross Kinnaman, overall Skiesta chairman, presided at the public-address mike, calling events and giving a running account of the three-ring circus on the slope. Announcements of prize winners and awards were made by Kinnaman Sunday evening at the dance in the civic club.

"Out of the gliding, weaving pattern of ridiculously costumed skiers on the slope, many impressions stood out. To name only a few destined for the local hall of fame: Herb Weiss' sawed-off skis, red skirt, and coy coiffure fashioned from a mop; Fred Kalbach's one-man fire department complete with snow-propelled, paddle-wheel siren attached to skis; the dramatic entrance of the three near-naked savages who came whooping out of the woods; Ozzie (Earl) Swickard's suave detachment in an impeccable tux during a downhill schuss; be-splintered, be-bandaged Jim Coon poling mightily with crutches; Elise Cunningham's graceful maneuvers and complete unconcern with her billowing skirts and ruffled pantalettes as she descended the length of the slope in a series of graceful stem-christies.

Images from the first Skiesta, Sawyer's Hill, Febraury 29, 1948. In the smaller photo, Old King Cole, carved from a mountain of snow, welcomes celebrants to the Skiesta.

"Early disappearance of the sun gave the three braves cause to shudder but kept the snow from turning unduly wet in the comparatively mild temperature.

"Mary Huston's food committee steadily dished out beans, hot dogs, donuts, and coffee during the early part of the afternoon (the lunch cost 50 cents). Assisting her were Elise Cunningham, Mrs. Les Seeley, Mrs. Arthur Hemmendinger, Mr. and Mrs. D.J. Shaad, and Jim Bridge.

"Old King Cole, carved out of a mountain of snow by Bill Broome and assorted apprentices, looked on with approval while numerous youngsters clamored over his legs to perch three abreast on his capacious lap. Marking the entrance to the slope were a genial snow host and hostess. Balloons strung between trees added to the festive air. Mammoth-sized balloons were rolled downhill by skiers in one of the contests.

"Credit for decorations went to Broome, his wife, and numerous other assistants including Mr. and Mrs. Ted Belchar, Mr. and Mrs. Don Schell, Miss Evelyn Kline, Herb Weiss, Mr. and Mrs. Ross L. Kinnaman, Alan Robinson, and Don Gibson.

"Jim Coon and Herb Weiss were judged to have the best costumes in the men's class; Mrs. Kinnaman and Becky Bradford won in the women's class. The team of Joe Stark and Ben Hayward took the leap-frog race. Clarence West came in first and Marty Noland second in the balloon race. First prizes in the three uphill schusses went to Bill Stein, Joe Stark, and Don Johnstone; second prizes went to Alan Robinson, Vernon Struebing, and Bill Doyle. Six-year-old Nick King, son of Mr. and Mrs. L.D.P. King, and Richard Burrias, 8, son of Mr. and Mrs. Stanley W. Burrias, came in first and second, respectively, in the downhill race for kids. Winners in the four musical chair heats were John Well, John Orndoff, Vernal Josephson, and Don Gibson. Prizes for the biggest sitz-marks were voted to Jean Parks and Ben Hayward. Tiano Sporting Goods, the local sports shop, donated two wax kits, four ski carriers, four pairs of liners, six goggles, three pairs of climbers, and three cans of base coat as prizes."

Skiers enjoy the first Skiesta by satirizing a beginners' ski class.

Thus, "Skiesta," a zany finale to the ski season, was born.

Ultimately, winter succumbed to a Rocky Mountain spring, often given to gray moods, gusty winds, and fits of rain, even spitting snow. The ropes and moveable parts on the tows were stored, skis were stacked in closet corners, and ski club members immediately began to plan for a major improvement at Sawyer's Hill: a new ski lodge.

The Ski Lodge

The ski club, like many local organizations, functioned as closely to a free enterprise business arrangement as possible. Operational costs for the ski club were paid for by membership fees, daily lift tickets, and uncounted hours of volunteer labor, but to build a ski lodge, the club would have to approach the AEC for the funds and the land.

Mary Huston's food committee steadily dished out beans, hot dogs, donuts, and coffee during the early part of the afternoon (the lunch cost 50 cents).

Los Alamos was a company town, owned by the government, and maintained by the Zia Company. There was no private ownership of homes or businesses. Every necessity and amenity that comprises a community was funded and built by the government. The process of administration was complicated.

The Town Council could only recommend and negotiate with the AEC for the needs of the community through the manager from an office in Santa Fe who was the spokesman and contact person with the AEC in Washington.

In a letter dated May 7, 1948, AEC manager Carroll L. Tyler delegated the first major, self-governing power to the Town Council. He stated that those powers delegated, in effect, were those regulating all traffic in the town and residential areas. The move was a commitment to adhere to his proposed policy to permit Los Alamos to be a self-governing community "insofar as possible," as he felt the community was organized for handling and efficiently administrating them.

To bring in needed businesses vital to a growing community, an organization called the Community Council Inc. hired a business manager, who advertised for bids and let contracts to the concessions that served the best interests of the town.

In fact, Los Alamos was featured in the 59th series of articles on America's most colorful cities that appeared in a 1948 issue of the *Saturday Evening Post*: In part it read, "here, where the curving Rio Grande skirts the high mesas of the Jemez Mountains, the most remarkable town in the world is trying to be born...the crowded, dusty, clamoring little community of Los Alamos, which considers itself the capital of the Atomic Age, and hopes to prove itself a model of planning of the future.... It has no cemetery, no jail, no courts and as yet, no fixed status in the legal machinery of New Mexico or the United States.... 'I almost never ask anyone from the outside to visit us on Thursdays,' one famous hostess of the town remarked ... 'the boys always seem to pick Thursdays for their noisiest experiments.' ...the average age of the town council is in the early thirties, and it is normal for crew haircuts to turn up in highly responsible positions.... It is your town, the property of the taxpayers of the United States, and one of these days you are going to be called upon to do some thinking and deciding about this $500 million investment which you cannot do without, but which you may fear you can't afford."

The new ski lodge at Sawyer's Hill. Many of the volunteers who built it enjoy a party inside the newly constructed lodge.

Indeed, the main business of Los Alamos was the Laboratory. At an orientation talk to a group of summer students on July 27, 1948, Director Norris E. Bradbury outlined the primary objectives of the Laboratory, which were twofold, he said.

First, its purpose was to investigate the many ideas for use of fissionable materials in weapons.

Second, the purpose of the Laboratory was basic research, which Bradbury said was the life blood of scientific progress, without which work would become a mere cleaning up of details.

As part of the Laboratory philosophy, Bradbury emphasized the need to "overcome compartmentalization...segregation of divisions and groups so that one member knows little or nothing of what another division or group is doing."

When Bradbury was asked about the permanence of the Laboratory, he cited the $100 million program for rebuilding the Tech Area and the long-range $7 million housing program.

Los Alamos was growing. Certainly, there was a need for a new ski lodge at Sawyer's Hill. Through the efforts of Herb Weiss, Jim Coon, and Beckie Bradford, the AEC authorized $6,800 for the construction of the lodge, which was to be erected at the foot of Sawyer's Hill.

Elizabeth Orndoff demonstrates good rope tow technique at Sawyer's Hill.

Designed by club member John Suttman, the planned structure, 20 by 40 feet in area, would look out upon the ski slope. Club members said they would volunteer their efforts to build the outdoor fireplace and the flagstone terrace.

However, ownership of the lodge and the land would be retained by the Los Alamos Project Management from whom the ski club would lease the facilities.

On weekends, Sawyer's Hill buzzed with large work parties, 50 or more people. Crews teamed up to cut brush off the main slope, the north trail, and the tow path; to install the tow pulleys; to clean up the motor shack area; to level the tow path areas; and to dig under stumps, 6 feet in diameter, so Seeley could blow them out with explosives. A winter's supply of fireplace wood was split and stacked. Flagstone for the patio was hauled and set. Doors that wouldn't close were planed, and final coats of paint were applied.

Meanwhile, Neil Davis searched for wicker furniture for the lodge. Jim Bridge had already forged the heavy fireplace andirons. Mary Huston had her list of needs: curtain rods and curtains, a black beauty wood burner for the kitchen, two Coleman lamps, and large ski posters from Sweden and Switzerland to decorate the walls. By fall, the new lodge was ready for occupancy.

"When these things are done," said a ski club bulletin, "we can call on the Indians for a snow dance."

Not only did the season open with a new ski lodge, there were the additions of a volunteer ski patrol and a professional ski school.

The Los Alamos Ski Patrol, first organized by Les Seeley, was in operation with John Orndoff as captain (the word "leader" was shunned as it suggested "the Fuehrer," which was the chilling word of Nazi Germany). The ski patrol consisted of ten volunteer members who were trained in Red Cross first aid and rescue techniques. Buzz Bainbridge, who operated the Hyde Park Ski Area near Santa Fe in 1946–47 and had organized a racing team that often trained at Sawyer's Hill, conducted the ski competency test.

According to Orndoff, "Bainbridge took us to the top of Sawyer's Hill and said, 'Now snowplow straight down the mountain.' That was the fastest snowplow I ever did!"

Supported by the ski club, the ski patrol assumed responsibility for safety and accident problems at Sawyer's Hill. "We were issued morphine styrettes by the local hospital doctors," said Orndoff.

When the Santa Fe Ski Basin opened for business that year, "There were very few qualified patrolmen in the local area," said Orndoff, "so, shortly after our National Ski Patrol unit was established, we ran the ski patrol at the Basin for a couple of years. As volunteers, our families could ski for free." But at Sawyer's Hill, the ski patrollers preferred to pay for their ski memberships and to offer their services on a purely volunteer basis.

Volunteers work to prepare Sawyer's Hill for another winter, October 1948.

When the ski club asked Bainbridge and his wife to conduct the ski school, they happily agreed. Thanks to the ski patrol, who often stopped out-of-control skiers and suggested they take a ski lesson that cost $2 for a two-hour session, Bainbridge said, "the money was like cream on the coffee, we loved it. We didn't give the club a penny but kept it all, came home with a pocketfull of dollars."

Bainbridge recalled, "It was kind of a thrill coming to Los Alamos. We had to stop at the gate, get passes, and were warned not to lose them. We'd pray we'd get out." Mostly, he said, "we were impressed with the spirit of the Los Alamos skiers."

Five years of bonanza snowfalls helped make Sawyer's Hill one of the oldest ski areas in the state, a favorite spot for families to congregate on weekends.

Even during the summers, work parties were large family affairs. Many volunteers were needed to help clear the land, which was a laborious operation. According to Gene Tate, the work was done by hand using a two-man crosscut saw. An ax was used to trim the tree branches. Then the logs were rolled down the mountain.

J.O. Johnson said, "The whole family was up there with picnic baskets.... Mommy and the babies, little kids hauling branches off into the woods, dogs ... people running around the slopes ... trees crashing down. It was a miracle we didn't lose anyone. This is the way we cut slopes at Sawyer's."

In fact, when the North Slope was cut in 1954–55, Tom Putman remembered a large pine tree about two feet in diameter that had been felled and sawed into 10- and 20-foot lengths. They decided to roll the logs down toward the side of the slope, but the logs never turned. Instead they rolled directly toward an astonished crowd of people who were running to escape the avalanche of tumbling timber. "It was a little scary," Putnam added.

One slope that was cleared quickly became dubbed "Wood's Folley," said Diven. "Jim Wood wanted a racing trail so one could do short, quick turns, but the trail was so steep and narrow that very few people could use it. You almost came to a turn and had to stop to do a kick turn to make a turn," she said. But the problem was recognized, and the trail was widened.

Although the ski club discouraged naming trails or slopes after people, another trail that could never shed its moniker was Jones Trail, named after Wes Jones, who reportedly broke his leg twice on the same trail.

The zest for skiing took a creative turn at Sawyer's Hill when in 1951, a few folks decided to introduce night skiing on Wednesday nights. A generator was acquired and about six flood lights were mounted on trees from the Red Tree on down.

An unidentified woman and Jim Coon saw a felled tree for fireplace fuel. Jim Wood is standing. For many determined skiers, working at Sawyer's Hill had become a summer habit.

When the moon was bright, tree shadows were cast on the snow, which caused some concern. James (Stretch) Fretwell said that was the spooky part about night skiing. "There was a question in your mind about that shadow.... Is that a shadow on the snow or is that a tree umbrella where there is only grass?"

Putman recalled that it was difficult to see people. He was narrowly missed by a person who skied out from behind the trees and crossed the front of his skis.

Orndoff said, "I remember night skiing only once, and I ran into a steel slalom pole." Virginia Wynne Barela, then a teenager, remembers one evening of night skiing when she was surprised by icy snow beneath a tree. She slipped, tearing the ligaments in her foot. "One ski made a half turn with my foot in it," she said. "In those days we didn't have safety bindings ... only a safety strap ... a piece of leather tied to your bindings and to your ankle so in case your ski came off, it wouldn't fly down the hill and nail someone."

Ginnie Bell remembered, "It was so cold and the bumps became holes and the holes became bumps and forget the whole thing."

For Joan Coon, night skiing was "OK" if the moon was out. She said her main memory was hearing "Bill Jarmie yodelling as he went flying down the mountain."

But as the years passed, there was little to yodel about, as poor snow conditions damped the initial excitement of skiing at Sawyer's

Hill. Rocks were a frequent hazard on an average day, according to Sam Bame, a former ski club president.

Dale Holm remembers walking the slopes and throwing off a rock as big as a fist, a serious hazard.

Frustration with skiing conditions peaked during the winter of 1956–57. Sawyer's Hill was opened only seven days that year, and skiers encountered black mud, yellow straw, and scattered patches of melting snow. One group of determined skiers, disgusted with the iffy ski conditions at Sawyer's Hill, decided to scout the mountains to find an alternative ski area.

The Holm party searches for better snow conditions on Pajarito Mountain, March 1957. Shown from left are Tom Putnam, Stretch Fretwell, Pat Fretwell, and Bill Jarmie.

"The slope faced east," said Fretwell, "so the morning sun cooked everything out on it."

Holm said, "There just wasn't the capability at Sawyer's to do anything really significant. If there was to be a decent ski area, it would have to have a north-facing slope. In our mind there was pay dirt in a higher altitude. We knew about the pipeline road and knew there was something up there."

In fact, Hup Wallis, an instructor at the Ranch School, had cleared a small hill near Camp May, located just seven miles west of town, for skiing. During the winter, the boys and their horses, pulling sleds loaded with equipment, trudged through deep snow to spend a week or weekend at Camp May to ski. Perc King, who skied there often with Enrico Fermi, verified that good snow usually existed in the region into late spring.

"We had to confirm the snow conditions ourselves," said Tom Putnam, so a strategy session to check out the highest point in the county took place in Bill Jarmie's home where Fretwell papered the dining room table with topography maps of the Pajarito area. "To see the beauty of the mountain for developing ski slopes was exciting," said Jarmie. "We were astonished at its potential as a ski area."

An exploration day to check out the snow cover was scheduled for March 17, 1957. Driving World War II jeeps with chains on all four wheels, the large group of explorers, thirteen in all, split into two smaller parties. The plan was to approach the Camp May area from two different directions.

Orndoff said that Dale Holm, Tom Putnam, Bill Jarmie, and Stretch and Pat Fretwell drove up the present ski hill road, which

A summer search party hikes near Pajarito Mountain and studies a map of the area. The party includes the Orndoff family, Tom Putnam, Dale Holm, Stretch Fretwell, an unidentified man, and Bill Bernard.

was then a segment of the pipeline road. Meanwhile, his party (Bill Bernard, Steve Nichols, the Orndoff family and a neighbor) followed the pipeline road from the other end to Sawyer's Saddle at the head of the Quemazon Canyon.

Both parties encountered snow. Party one abandoned the jeeps at the bottom of the hill now called Nevershine. Charged with renewed excitement, they put on their skis (though not cross-country skis) and hiked nearly two miles to the present location of the Big Mother lift where the Ranch School boys skied.

Orndoff's party was able to reach its destination and had only to hike a short distance to reach the Ranch School slope.

The explorers were jubilant!

"There was nearly four feet of snow, and we hadn't skied at Sawyer's for nearly a month," said Holm.

"That was discovery day," said Fretwell. "Soon the word spread that there was snow at Pajarito."

Inspired by the prospect of a better ski area, the young, energetic explorers lobbied the ski club membership to move the ski operation from Sawyer's Hill to Pajarito Mountain, but some members were reluctant to vacate Sawyer's Hill.

Gene Tate, the ski club president at the time, was least enthusiastic to move to Pajarito. He had worked long hours to maintain the equipment. He even spent Thanksgiving day shingling the roof on the tow shack!

Three pioneers of skiing in New Mexico: Mal Wallis, Buzz Bainbridge, and Ernie Blake at Santa Fe Ski Basin in 1956. Wallis started a ski racing program in Los Alamos, Bainbridge played an instrumental role in the development of Santa Fe Ski Basin, and Ernie Blake, in 1956, was the operator of Santa Fe Ski Basin. Today, Blake's name is synonymous with Taos ski area because of his role in its development.

Fretwell thought that it was surprisingly easy to persuade the members to move, but one chief concern troubled him. Because of limited time, there would be minimal clearing of the slopes for the first season of skiing at Pajarito. "If we had good snow at Sawyer's, everyone would say, 'Oh gee, we should have stayed where we were," he said.

Robert Thorn, ski club president in 1957–58, didn't think the membership needed much convincing to move the ski area. "It seems to me," he said, "it was a resounding vote in favor of doing that."

Tate acknowledged, "A nucleus of people decided that was the thing to do. They were highly motivated and got things done."

Thorn agreed. "I have to give credit where credit is due. The move to Pajarito Mountain was due to the pioneers of the club."

SKI RENTAL
TOW TICKETS
EMERGENCY
FIRST
AID
AMERICAN RED CROSS
USA
USA

Part Three

Pajarito Mountain

Pajarito Mountain—The Move

Set against a southwestern sky of cobalt blue, Pajarito Mountain rises to an elevation of 10,441 feet. Today, the ski area is spread across 730 acres of mostly intermediate to expert terrain. From a great distance, the ski slopes, cut through the pines and aspens, can be seen, in summer, as grasslands where elk herds roam and, in winter, as snowfields where skiers flock.

Accommodations for the skiers include five chair lifts, a ski school, ski-equipment rentals, a cafeteria, and a day lodge. The ski club's annual membership numbers about 3,000, a sharp increase from the 365 members in 1957.

In the beginning, many of the volunteers, a group of people enthusiastic and committed to building a ski area, never imagined that their venture would grow into a $1 million-a-year, non-profit business. In fact, in 1985, Bob Thorn estimated that volunteers donated approximately 8,000 man-hours per year to the mountain.

Pajarito Mountain in the background, with Western Area housing in the foreground.

Dale Holm said, "I thought that perhaps one lift would be it for the mountain. But it exceeds my wildest expectations."

John Orndoff said, "It's hard to believe, looking at what we have now and what it was. It was kind of amazing to have skiing that first year. I worked my tail off."

Bill Jarmie said, "It's wonderful to see how much volunteer effort and energy helped keep this place going year after year."

The volunteers gave little thought to how their working together, on Pajarito Mountain, would evolve into an esprit de corps that would lead to lifelong friendships.

Rene Prestwood recalled, "You couldn't keep me off the mountain. See, that mountain is more than just a ski hill. For many of us, it was kind of a way of life."

The Pajarito Ski Area story began in the spring of 1957. The ski club embraced change, and men and women of all ages and from all occupations engaged in an heroic effort to move the ski area from Sawyer's Hill to Pajarito Mountain, where the north-facing slope promised deeper snow, another 1,000 feet of vertical ski slopes, and a longer ski season. The list of jobs to be done that first season was staggering! The area had no rope tows, cleared ski slopes, lodge, outhouses, or parking lot. Nor did it have a passable road in winter.

However, before real work could begin on the mountain, the ski club had to obtain a "use permit" for the land. To secure that land permit, John Rogers worked with Paul Wilson, then the manager of the local AEC office. The Los Alamos Ski Club operated under that permit until September 8, 1961, when it signed a contract with the AEC to lease 101 acres of land for $325 a year for 50 years.

"There was tremendous support by the AEC," Rogers said. "They were overwhelmingly cooperative."

The partnership between the citizens of Los Alamos and the AEC drew its mandate from the spirit of General Groves, who was determined to support recreation for Los Alamos, a secluded town resolutely dependent on the government. That dependency still existed in 1957. The development of recreational facilities such as ball fields, tennis courts, a skating rink, horse stables, hiking trails, a golf course, and parks was a result of that cooperative effort.

A few "old time" ski club members expressed concern that this arrangement might be misunderstood, and they thought perhaps it should not be disclosed in this book. Yet, they were the first to say that, like many of the recreational facilities in town, the development of the ski area at Pajarito Mountain would have been extremely difficult, if not impossible, without the cooperation of the AEC, the Zia Company, and the Laboratory. That support was reflected in the development of the Camp May Road.

In the beginning, many of the volunteers, a group of people enthusiastic and committed to building a ski area, never imagined that their venture would grow into a $1 million-a-year, non-profit business. In fact, in 1985, Bob Thorn estimated that volunteers donated approximately 8,000 man-hours per year to the mountain.

The Story of Camp May Road

"In our excitement about finding such good snow in the Camp May area," Tom Putnam said, "we wanted to encourage the county to develop it for a year-round, recreational area." Thus, a plan to improve the Camp May Trail was initiated by the ski club. By this time, the Los Alamos Town Council had been superseded by a three-member County Commission. To strengthen the ski club's proposal to the county commissioners, Putnam said that a letter, which was sent to all the organizations in town, asked for support and suggestions as to how the area could be developed for outdoor activities.

In response to the ski club's request, a special County Commission meeting was held, which allowed the public an opportunity to review the proposal to improve the road to Camp May and to develop it as an all-year recreational area. According to the *Santa Fe New Mexican*, the public responded favorably. The article stated: "Representatives of the Los Alamos Ski Club, Girl Scouts, Boy Scouts, Pajarito Field Archers, and interested citizens all gave an enthusiastic nod to the project. There wasn't one dissenter in the audience."

In order to fund the Camp May Trail project, the County Commission unanimously passed a resolution that sought permission from the State Attorney General's office and the comptroller to withdraw the balance of $3,500 from the county road fund. They also voted to draw another $11,500 from the miscellaneous salary item. These monies would pay the salaries of teenagers hired to work in a summer program aimed at clearing timber and building culverts on the Camp May Road. An additional $8,000, already budgeted for the work, would be used to cover the expenses of the heavy rental equipment needed to grade the road.

Though the Camp May Road and proposed recreational area were considered worthwhile projects, there were opponents. The *Santa Fe New Mexican* reported: "Camp May Trail Program Hits Snag.... A sour apple has cropped up in the barrel as far as the summer work program and road work on the Camp May trail, despite the community support shown at the special meeting last week to discuss all aspects of the proposed program."

"The cost was $1,200," said Rogers. "Imagine! Six inches of gravel over 4.3 miles for only $1,200."

The article further stated that some people who apparently disagreed with the decision reached by the county commissioners concerning the Camp May Trail complained to the attorney general's office about the situation. In turn, this complaint not only challenged a legal issue but cast a bitter mood between friends and foes of the project.

Two county commissioners, James Teare and James Gittings, thought that perhaps the people who objected to the project hadn't understood the limitations on the county road funds and the state secondary road fund. The *New Mexican* reported that Teare and Gittings felt betrayed and perplexed by residents who declined the opportunity to speak their piece at a public meeting called for that one purpose, but who would deliberately go behind their backs to undermine a project enthusiastically supported by a large number of organizations and clubs.

The legal question was complicated. Could the county build or improve a road that was not the property of the county but whose use was subject to the control of the AEC?

The AEC, for security reasons, could not deed nor dedicate the road to the county, but the AEC could lease the road to the county. The state was concerned about the legality of the project, which could affect all road work in Los Alamos County. Until the AEC, the attorney general, and the state comptroller settled the question, 70 teenagers, who had enrolled in the summer work program to clear the Camp May Road, sat idle.

Paul Wilson, area manager of the AEC, quickly responded to the situation. By cutting through the official red tape, permission to use the road was granted to the county. The project was saved, and the teenagers went to work.

Ski club members, delighted with the outcome, executed the initial survey of the road. Dale Holm said, "Bob Douglas was the brains behind the survey crew. Trained in surveying, he used a hand-held transit to survey."

The survey map indicated those areas that were too steep and outlined those areas that needed to be changed. Holm said that the county then used that map to negotiate a contract with the Santa Fe Construction Company to grade the road. The contract was let for a little under $7,500.

By mid-August heavy equipment rumbled along the Camp May Trail. Holm doesn't know why the very steep pitch at the beginning of the road was created. The old road was reconfigured about mid-way up the mountain. At Nevershine Hill, the road was graded in such a fashion as to give cars a running chance to reach the top on snowy, icy, or muddy days. Finally, a six-inch-deep layer of gravel was spread along the 4.3 miles of graded road that stretched from its beginning to the base of the Pajarito ski area.

"The cost was $1,200," said Rogers. "Imagine! Six inches of gravel over 4.3 miles for only $1,200."

A bit of Camp May Road is visible after the Cerro Grande fire of May 2000. The fire revealed the steepness of Los Alamos Canyon.

The official opening of the road took place on September 19, 1957. The festivities drew a large crowd of county and state officials, representatives from the Democratic and Republican parties, members of the Los Alamos Ski Club, and other club representatives. Since Paul Wilson's mediation made the road possible, it was fitting that he cut the ceremonial red ribbon. Wilson told the *New Mexican* that he felt the road was not only a credit to the county but also to the general area of the project. Dinner at the Golf Club concluded the celebration.

"It was the only county road," said Stretch Fretwell. "The rest of the roads were taken care of by the Zia Company and the AEC."

County Commissioner Bob Thorn, who championed the ski club's move to Pajarito Mountain, said, "I did the best I could to try to improve the road up to the ski area...and of course the AEC was much more influential in those days than was the county."

"Skiers of the Hill, Arise!"

In a race with the calendar, the ski club had only seven months to complete the formidable task of moving the ski area from Sawyer's Hill to Pajarito Mountain. Work parties met on Saturdays and Sundays from dawn until dark. They set their goals: clear natural meadows for the first ski slopes, cut the paths for the rope tows, upgrade and install the engines and tow lines, grade a parking lot, and last but not least, move a building to the area for a lodge and install a couple of single-hole outhouses.

Much of the timber in 1957 was cut with axes and bow saws.

By August nearly 300 man-hours had been put to the effort. Still, teams of three or four people were needed to fell the trees, to be followed by more teams of 10 or 20 people to strip, buck, and stack the slash, either to be burned before winter or piled in cribs to be hauled off.

Bill Jarmie wrote a memo that was sent to the ski club membership. It called for more manpower. It began:

"Skiers of the Hill, Arise! You have nothing to lose but the doubtful pleasure of skiing on rocks, stumps, and beer cans."

Jarmie's memo ended with this inducement:

"Work parties will probably continue every weekend for the 15 or 16 left until winter. Many new faces have appeared on the scene, and newcomers are particularly welcome. These high woods are especially beautiful with the recent rains, and we hope many of you will be able to come up and enjoy them while discovering muscles you have forgotten about. There is a great deal of work still to be done, so please, if you can, come and help! ... Here's to a 3/4 mile schuss...."

Volunteers rallied to the memo, but bad weather plagued their efforts. Summer rains forced delays. Thorn said, "It was the wettest August we'd ever had and made it difficult to get any work done."

Annoyed by delays, the volunteers also faced many difficulties such as cutting a large stand of timber on a slope now called Lumberyard.

Thorn and Bill Wood used a two-man chain saw, which was big and difficult to maneuver, to cut the timber. The main work was done with axes and bow saws. People came up with bow saws with red handles and Swedish steel blades. "That is what we used to cut timber," said Thorn. "We were cutting very long lengths of timber, and there was no way we could get that much timber bucked-up in the fall, so we laid the timber on the ground as smooth as we could."

"That first winter we had no problem about sliding on those trees," said Thorn. "That is probably because we didn't have enough skiers, plus we had an awful lot of snow." However, when the snow conditions were poor, a ski could slip down into the logs. It didn't take long before the ski club, encouraged by the Forest Service, removed the corduroy of timber.

In early October 1957, just as work parties prepared to transport a ski lodge to Pajarito, wind and snow lashed at the mountain, creating miserable working conditions.

"We moved a Gamma 2 building that was built by the Army for the Laboratory's use up there," said John Rogers. "The events of moving it were fascinating."

According to Stretch Fretwell, the structure, which stood on the southeast side of Ashley Pond, was declared surplus when the tech area buildings were torn down. "We removed all struts and purtenances underneath the building," said Fretwell.

Thorn added, "It was given to the ski club, providing the ski club removed it. There were work parties at night to cut the building in half."

Fretwell said there wasn't a foundation for the building at Pajarito. "We were behind schedule and running out of time."

What to do?

Aspen trees became the solution. "We cut nearby aspen trees… big ones…about 18 inches in diameter and laid them down in the mud," said Fretwell.

Once the aspen tree foundation was in place, Bob Waterman, a local contractor and enthusiastic skier, had agreed to haul the building up the mountain and set it on the foundation of logs.

"But we got caught in the snow before we were ready," said John Rogers.

"There we were with the lodge in the middle of the road," said Thorn. "The lodge needed to be moved to its final location, but three feet of snow on the ground and three feet of frozen mud under the snow provided a challenging obstacle."

A grader was brought in to plow the snow off the road, but the operator hadn't expected the frozen ground to thaw.

"He buried the grader in the mud and wouldn't go back up there. The snow had to be hand shoveled," said Holm. "Waterman took that building up there on a corduroy road that we built."

Fretwell said, "He dropped that building on those logs, and it settled and creaked and cracked." In order to level the building, car jacks were used to lift the building so that shims could be placed beneath it.

Rogers said, "I remember working in the mud, wet, cold ... mud up to my knees…and jacking that building up with these huge jacks

An Army structure—cut in half and moved from Ashley Pond to Pajarito Mountain—serves as the first ski lodge.

Deep snow hinders the efforts as two halves of the Gamma 2 building are installed on a log foundation.

and putting rocks underneath it. After that, Thorn and I ordered insulated boots. We weren't going to get mired in all that muck again."

"I remember that day very well," said Fretwell. "We worked late into the night, snaking aspen logs down to the building by using a cable attached to a winch on my jeep." In the process, a loop of cable wrapped around his front wheel so when he backed-up his jeep, the cable cut the brake line. "Driving down Pajarito Mountain with no brakes…I shifted gears very often and very carefully," he said.

"Conditions made it very dismal and hard to do the work and only for the spirit of the people engaged in the effort could it ever have been accomplished," said Thorn.

Once the building was in place, Carl Buckland built the staircase and finished the interior. Long after sunset and late into the night, Buckland worked.

"I put windows in the lodge on the south side and made French doors at night by a Coleman lantern," said Buckland. Fretwell dubbed him the "skiing carpenter."

"The building would creak and crack but was quite usable," said Fretwell.

In a ski club newsletter dated April 9, 1958, Thorn wrote, "The lodge will have to pass a Zia building inspection this summer. Hopefully, the foundation will meet the requirements with very little additional labor."

Meanwhile, work teams, hampered by knee-deep snow and cold that cut to the bone, struggled to clear slopes. By November 1957, the

No. 1 tow path was ready. The engine—which had been acquired from Hyde Park in Santa Fe and had powered the north tow at Sawyer's Hill—was installed. The rope was strung.

The No. 1 rope tow was 2,300 feet long, and the terrain had a vertical rise of 605 feet. The No. 1 rope tow was considered the longest rope tow in the southwest, if not the world. Thorn and Fretwell recalled that the length of that rope tow was accidental.

"A bull wheel was installed on a slight aspen tree, which was probably only 8 or 10 inches in diameter," said Fretwell. "The rope was then attached to that bull wheel. The crew went home happy that the main tow was done."

"I put windows in the lodge on the south side and made French doors at night by a Coleman lantern," said Buckland. Fretwell dubbed him the "skiing carpenter."

Thorn said, "Snow came along and, of course, the aspen tree immediately fell over. We went 300 feet up that same line and found a big fir tree, the only fir tree in that line which could withstand the tensions of the rope. We were able to fasten a pulley onto that tree and carry the rope up that much farther...so, that tree was a very lucky thing."

Fretwell thought that tree was a survivor of the great fire that swept through Pajarito Mountain in the late 1800s.

In November and December of 1957, winter clung to the mountain and promised an early ski season. In fact, volunteers staggered through 70 inches of snow to finish clearing a small area for the beginning skiers. It would be Christmas before the Beginner's Rope Tow No. 2 was finished. The rope was 1,155 feet long, and the terrain had a 250-foot vertical rise. Finally, an International Harvester, four-cylinder engine, which was used at Sawyer's Hill to drive the big tow, was installed.

"Part of that rope tow was made in C-Shop," said Fretwell. "The sheaves were cut out of solid plates and machined...it was a 'government job' and somebody wrote a work order for it...it went through."

The volunteers had met their goals. In place was a passable road, parking lot, lodge, two rope tows, some cleared ski slopes, and outhouses.

"It was pretty primitive by any standards, but we could start skiing," said Thorn. "We didn't quit skiing until the first of April ...there was too much snow for the rope tow...it was spring-time skiing, and the ropes got wet and started slipping in the drive sheave." Opening day at the new ski area was November 12, 1957. That first season, 365 members of the ski club enjoyed 169 inches of snow and 38 days of skiing. Immediately following that ski season, a membership meeting of the Los Alamos Ski Club was held to discuss a program for summer development of the Pajarito ski area.

Tax-Exempt Status

When the Sawyer's Hill Ski Tow Association was formed with 150 charter members in 1944, the Sawyer's Hill property was owned by the Manhattan Project, as was Los Alamos. As far as the state of New Mexico was concerned, Los Alamos didn't exist except as a federal reservation. After the end of the war in 1945, that situation changed. The Manhattan Project ended, and the Laboratory became the Los Alamos Scientific Laboratory, operated by the University of California but funded and governed by the Atomic Energy Commission, a federal agency.

In 1949, Los Alamos became part of the state of New Mexico by drawing land from portions of Sandoval, Santa Fe, and Rio Arriba counties to form Los Alamos County, the 32nd and smallest county in the state. Shortly after, the Sawyer's Hill Ski Tow Association decided it was time to become an official part of the state of New Mexico. By 1954, the Los Alamos Ski Club was formed and incorporated under the laws of the state of New Mexico.

On October 9, 1958, the ski club applied for a federal tax exemption under section 501 (c)(7) of the Internal Revenue Code. This application was denied by the IRS since section 501(c)(7) applied to private clubs, and under IRS rules private clubs must hold a liquor license. The ski club did not hold a liquor license nor did it want one.

The ski club then reapplied, in October 1960, for exemption under Internal Revenue Code section 501(c)(3). That code allowed for a tax exemption for religious, charitable, scientific, and educational organizations. This application was accepted on November 18, 1960, after the ski club amended their articles of incorporation to more nearly reflect the IRS requirements. The exemption not only applied to federal tax, but because of New Mexico statutes, organizations under section 501(c)(3) were exempt from state income tax and gross receipts tax.

In order to follow the rules of the exemption, the ski club was required to follow some fairly stringent guidelines. The ski club agreed to the following:

1. Restrict membership in the ski club to those individuals either living or employed in Los Alamos County or retired from businesses operating in Los Alamos County.
2. Set rates for skiing and other services that did not unfairly compete with those charged by other skiing facilities in the area.
3. Provide public access to the ski-area facilities at nominal cost.
4. Continue educational and service programs at the ski area as defined in the original application, namely ski patrol and ski school.
5. Not advertise or obtain news media coverage in order to compete or appear to compete with commercial ski areas within the state.

In the fall of 1993, the IRS conducted an audit of the Los Alamos Ski Club to determine if the ski club continued to meet the criteria of section 501(c)(3). Thus began a long, drawn-out series of negotiations between attorneys that, on October 28, 1996, resulted in the loss of the 501 (c) (3) exemption. The exempt status was changed to a 501(c)(4), which resulted in the ski club's still being exempt from federal and state income taxes but being required to collect state gross receipt taxes.

Growing Pains for Los Alamos

In February 1957, Los Alamos became an open town. After 14 years, people could come and go without a security pass. Many Los Alamos citizens had grown accustomed to the shield of security that protected them from outsiders. They felt vulnerable. Some expressed grave concern that the town would be vandalized by strangers, now able to freely enter the community. Parents often wondered if their teenagers, once corralled by the guard gates, were "on the Hill" or "off the Hill?"

But most people saluted the "tearing down of the fences" as a positive step taken to normalize a community built on the concept of being "temporary." Still, uncertainties about the future of the Laboratory and the town tugged at people's minds. Several task groups were formed to gather and assess information that would throw light on the future of Los Alamos.

Nevertheless, Los Alamos began to take on a look of permanence, and the late fifties and early sixties were a time of great change, both at the Laboratory and in the community.

Los Alamos began to take on a look of permanence, and the late fifties and early sixties were a time of great change, both at the Laboratory and in the community.

In 1959, the Laboratory's long-range plan to relocate the technical and administrative buildings from the townsite to South Mesa was near completion. Scientists were busy, not just with testing nuclear devices in Nevada, but with reactor research, nuclear propulsion in both submarine and space travel, and fundamental genetics. The Lab designed and built a whole-body counter for exhibit and demonstration at the Second Geneva Conference on the Peaceful Uses of Atomic Energy in the summer of 1958.

Meanwhile, Laboratory Director Norris Bradbury urged Lab managers to pay greater attention to public relations activities. By promoting the Laboratory through magazine articles or newspaper stories, and sending volunteers to speak at technical and nontechnical meetings around the country, he hoped to recruit technical staff and promote staff morale.

The Baby Boom, meanwhile, didn't bypass Los Alamos. In December 1959, the census counted 12,837 residents; of those, 6,950 were adults and 5,887 were children. Walnut Street won the distinction of having the most children: 291. Arizona and Alabama streets placed second and third, respectively, with over 200 children on each of these streets. The enrollment for the public schools was 4,078 children.

While the public schools strained to keep tempo with the growing population, families looked to the AEC to sell the government-owned homes into private ownership, such as had been done at Oak Ridge, Tennessee, and Richland, Washington.

However, the AEC held the position that it would not act to sell the government homes until private housing construction provided an adequate cushion of vacant houses and apartments in Los Alamos.

Family housing vacancies were essentially at zero, and the Laboratory could no longer promise new hires any kind of housing larger than a one-bedroom apartment.

Paul Wilson, local AEC area manager, estimated that the housing shortage in Los Alamos would continue until about 700 private homes were built, which would take about five years.

One measure for getting such homes built rested on the sale of Barranca Mesa lots to private individuals. In 1959, 69 lots had been sold, and an additional 47 lots would be up for sale the next year.

The town was also talking about the good news to homeowners that some banks would finance home builders. To further the cause for private home ownership, a plan to develop White Rock was sent to Washington for approval. In addition, the Laboratory released land for a proposed trailer park.

Meanwhile, 30 existing government-owned houses had been selected for improvement under the government's $1 million housing improvement program.

Lot no. 46 on Barranca Mesa, the first Los Alamos land transferred to private ownership, was sold to Mr. and Mrs. George N. White, Jr.

Houses built in Los Alamos and White Rock create an air of permanance and a semblance of a more normal community.

Some 60 Los Alamos pilots, who wanted to open the airport to private use, met heavy opposition from about 86 percent of the people who had homes near the airport. Numerous letters, pro and con, were sent to the local government, the Laboratory, and AEC officials. The County Commission appointed a committee to study the problem.

Even the future of Ashley Pond was being pondered. The question was "...whether the historic old puddle should be filled and used for a recreation area, restored and retained for beauty and sentiment's sake, or fixed up for swimming facilities." Again, a committee was appointed to investigate the possibilities.

Meanwhile, the spirit of volunteerism was active around the town. Ambitious members of the Los Alamos Sheriff's Posse built a sturdy log building on North Mesa. They celebrated its completion with a party on Christmas Eve and dubbed the new building "The Posse Shack."

At the old ski area at Sawyer's Hill, Kiwanis Club members worked on weekends to prepare the site for a new activity, Kamp Kiwanis. A YMCA survey indicated that more than 200 children were expected to attend the camp. Sadly, the volunteers faced a major project restoring the ski lodge, which had been widely damaged by vandals since the ski club abandoned it for Pajarito Mountain.

In preparation for the coming season, the ski club volunteers had cleared Lumberyard from the midway point to the top of the mountain. Fortunately, they were able to retrieve a tow shack from Sawyer's Hill, haul it up to Pajarito Mountain, and place it on a spot midway up Lumberyard. They were hampered by a wet, slick, muddy jeep road, and the project took almost a full day to complete and required two jeeps, a truck, an ax, and muscles. The tow shack housed a generator, transferred by the AEC from salvage to the ski club, and a motor for rope tow No. 3. The rope was 1,260 feet long, and the terrain had a 485-foot vertical rise.

In November, season tickets went on sale at $9 for students, $18 for adults, or $38 for families. The ski club offered ski classes taught by Tony and Inga Perry. The previous year 204 students had enrolled in the free ski school classes, sponsored by Los Alamos County under the auspices of the Los Alamos Ski Club, but students would now be charged 75 cents per class.

Seen in this 1958–59 photo are the Beginner's Slope, Lower Lumberyard, and a jeep road that zig-zags up to where Aspen Slope will soon be cut.

Saga of the Rope Tows

In the best of conditions, riding a rope tow, which required hand and shoulder strength, was difficult. Most skiers tied a rope tow gripper around their waist, then clamped the gripper onto the rope. "They were not particularly safe things, but they allowed us to get up the hill," said Dale Holm. "Every once in a while, people would get caught up with the gripper and with their jackets."

The rope tow shack is moved from Sawyer's Hill to Pajarito Mountain.

But the safety features in the rope tow system allowed people to escape from disaster. Bob Douglas installed the safety circuits for the tows, essential for the skiers protection.

"It was a neat system," said Bob Rohwer. "Douglas had the whole circuit diagram in his head. If a problem arose, Douglas could tell someone over the phone what wires to cut and what to expect."

The system worked like this. Posts were driven into the ground at intervals. On these posts were screen door hinges which, when closed, touched a screw that completed the ignition circuit on the rope tow engine. There was cable that ran alongside the rope tow. When a person got into trouble, such as falling or getting snagged on the rope, all he had to do was to reach out with a ski pole and whack the cable, which pulled the screen door hinge away from the screw, thus stopping the engine and the rope. The system, designed to be "fail safe," had double top gates, the second of which was on a separate electrical circuit.

Rohwer said there was even a safety gate at the top of the tow called a "people scraper." He said, "If your tow gripper jammed on the rope and the safety circuit didn't work, this people scraper would actually scrape you off the rope before you went through the sheave."

The tow shack is installed near a jeep road crossing Lumberyard.

When Kyle Thorn Wheeler was about age 7, she didn't know about the "people scraper." Wheeler recalled a time when her mittens got tangled in the rope, causing her to fall when she tried to step away from the rope. She was being dragged up the hill, and had it not been for John Rogers, who was riding behind her and hit the emergency safety stop, "I thought I'd be pulled up the rope into the trees and around the pulleys. It was a frightening experience." After that episode, she quit skiing until the T-bar lift was installed.

In fact, Wheeler wondered how the adults ever expected the young children to manage the tow and enjoy the sport. "Most of the time, children couldn't hold the rope up or didn't have the strength to make it to the top of the Beginner's Slope, even with a gripper," she said.

Only with the help of adults could the children ride the No. 3 rope tow that was installed in the summer of 1959.

Once the engine started, Nichols, with a pack strapped to his back containing a can of gasoline for the coffee cooker, water, coffee, and tools that might be needed for the day, clamped a gripper onto the rope for a tough ride up the mountain.

Tow No. 3 allowed skiers to reach the top of the mountain called Upper Lumberyard. Until the ski club could finance a Poma lift or a T-bar, tow No. 3 provided a short-term solution.

The rope tows were operated by Luther Rickerson and Wes Nichols. During the summer months, Rickerson and Nichols volunteered their services toward improving their rope tows. Rickerson overhauled the engines on tows No. 1 and 2. Nichols put in benches and improved the launching platform at tow No. 3. During the ski season, they were the only paid employees of the ski club.

Rickerson sold tickets, collected money, and checked membership patches and daily tickets. Throughout the day, he restarted the tow engines when they were stopped by skiers tripping the safety wires.

"Rickerson ruled with an iron fist," said Rene Prestwood. "You didn't want to leave a beer can around or he'd jump right on you."

Nichols, who operated tow No. 3, earned the reputation for having the most inaccessible pot of coffee in New Mexico.

Rickerson's and Nichols' winter weekends began at the break of dawn. They would meet at tow No. 1, where Nichols helped Rickerson start the engine.

"It was a huge commercial type engine that sat on sawhorses," said Nichols. "Rick would light a fire under the pan to warm up the oil. Along with a starter and battery, we still had to use a crank to get it started. It was really hard to turn."

Once the engine started, Nichols, with a pack strapped to his back containing a can of gasoline for the coffee cooker, water, coffee, and tools that might be needed for the day, clamped a gripper onto the rope for a tough ride up the mountain. Since Nichols was usually the first person to ride the rope tow, he had to dislodge the rope from hooks in the trees, because the ski patrol hung the rope on the hooks at the end of a skiing day.

"This prevented the rope from freezing to the ground," said Nichols. " As I went up the slope, I'd just flip the rope off the hooks. Usually the rope was snow covered. It would be a booger to dig out. That was rugged."

Long, steep rope tows at Pajarito Mountain challenged women, young children, and even the teenage racers who came from out of town for competitive races, giving local racers the advantage.

When he reached the end of tow No. 1, he skied along a jeep road that ran slightly downhill and across Lumberyard to tow No. 3, the Midway Station.

"The green shack, still on Lumberyard, is where you caught tow No. 3," said Prestwood. "Henry Filip and I would sometimes help him carry up his water."

Unlike Rickerson's engine, Nichols said, "I never had any trouble starting the commercial Dodge engine with six cylinders. It ran on gasoline and started quite easily by battery." But critters often littered the area, so Nichols had to perform housekeeping chores before he got his tow under way.

Prestwood said, "Pack rats would stack their pine cones and things right on top of the engine block. Nichols had to clean off all that pack rat stuff...the very next morning it was all back again."

"Yes," said Nichols. "Anything that was left free, even an 18-inch pipe wrench, they'd manage to drag somewhere and hide. They built nests all over everything...really a mess."

The rope on tow No. 3 was also hung on hooks in the trees. "This was a much steeper slope than tow No. 1," said Nichols. "It was quite a chore to get the rope down."

"That was a real bitch of a tow. It went straight up," said John Rogers.

"Hardly anybody made it up the first season," said J.O. Johnson. "There was only about eight feet of flat before the tow started up. There just wasn't enough time to get the rope tow gripper clamped before the steep climb began. Not many people could do it. Certainly no children."

Even the strongest skiers were challenged to ride the tow. "I don't know of anybody who could ride that tow without a gripper. I weighed 135 pounds, and the rope tow lifted me off the ground," said Bill Jarmie.

Nichols said that if people fell off the lift, they couldn't get back onto the rope, so it was necessary for them to hike over to the east side of Lumberyard, which was difficult because they had to climb through the deadfall timber that had been downed to clear the slope. When someone fell, someone else on the tow would trip the rope to stop it. Nichols said, "After the path was cleared, people would yell down the hill that all was clear, so I would start the lift. Only the expert skiers could ride, and very few women could get up."

"I had a long table, a bridge table, a 5-gallon coffee pot, and a pot of water for hot chocolate," said Nichols. "I'd dump the coffee grounds in the pot, pour in the water, and keep doing that all day long. By the middle of the afternoon, it really got strong. By then skiers needed something strong."

Because of the rope tow's length and vertical rise, and to solve the problem of the steep incline, Nichols reasoned that a launching shoot would add another eight or nine feet of flat surface before the rope began its ascent.

Trees that grew on site were cut and laid down to form a bed. Then smaller trees were placed transversely over the larger trees. The corduroy ramp was then covered with straw. Skiers now had 16 to 17 feet of flat surface to get their tow grippers clamped onto the rope.

"Once the ramp was extended, children could ride the rope," said Nichols, "but there had to be an adult in front or behind them to help them hold up the rope."

Joan Coon said, "Wes Nichols was so nice. If your kid fell off four times, he'd pick him up four times and put him back on."

Also, the rope tow gave local skiers an advantage. "Racers who came in from out-of-town couldn't ride that tow. They would get psyched out," said Trish Reed Taylor. "They would walk to get to the top of the mountain and the race course. We always won. We were good racers anyway, but those kids could not ride that rope tow."

Phyl Wallis said, "We felt so sorry for those kids. We had to help them hold the rope tow."

The New Mexico Ski Team at Sun Valley in 1961 or 1962 included racers from Los Alamos, Santa Fe, Albuquerque, and Taos.

Nichols said that the youngest child to ride the tow was Tony Wallis, son of Mal and Phyl. "Mal put him in a pack on his back…he'd ride up that tow and ski down with that boy."

Amenities and necessities were sparse at tow No. 3. Nichols did keep a supply of nylon rope for replacing broken tow-gripper ropes and a stash of tissues for skiers with drippy noses, but it was the hot cup of coffee or hot chocolate that won the appreciation of skiers who needed to warm-up and rest while sitting on a bench that Nichols had installed. To accommodate changing snow depths, Nichols fastened two posts at each end of the bench which were about eight inches above the ground. He attached devices on the four poles, so he could raise or lower the seat according to the snow level.

"I had a long table, a bridge table, a 5-gallon coffee pot, and a pot of water for hot chocolate," said Nichols. "I'd dump the coffee grounds in the pot, pour in the water, and keep doing that all day long. By the middle of the afternoon, it really got strong. By then skiers needed something strong."

Nichols displayed a coffee can posted with a sign that read, "Donations Appreciated." "Once in awhile somebody would put in a dollar," he said. "I never made money off it, but I never had to pay for coffee out of my pocket."

"While they were getting the toboggan ready… I think every one of them fell… I thought… Hey! No way am I going to ride with those characters. I skied down by myself."

Nichols named his establishment The Coffee Shop of Higher Altitude. He said that the name was a pun taken from the name of a coffee shop in town called The Coffee House of High Principles. That coffee house—founded by scientists James Tuck, Stan Ulam and John Holladay—was mentioned in an article written by San Francisco's columnist, Herb Caen. Though Nichols' Coffee Shop of Higher Altitude didn't find fame in the *San Francisco Chronicle*, it was popular with the skiers, numb with cold.

"Wes will always have a warm spot in my heart for that coffee house," said Johnson.

Even Nichols got to ski some each day when Keith Kelly, eventually joined by others, began the tradition of giving Nichols some free time. "He was the first to come by several times a day and say, 'Wes, go make a run.' So I did," said Nichols.

Nichols never missed a weekend running tow No. 3, even when a twisted knee posed a problem for him. If he put most of his weight on his good leg, he could ride the tow up the mountain, but he was unable to ski down at the end of the day.

Skiers enjoy a quick cup of coffee at Wes Nichols' Coffee Shop of Higher Altitude.

John Rogers, a ski patrolman, came to the rescue. "He'd load me in a toboggan…pull-up the chain…we'd schuss Lumberyard," said Nichols. "John told me, 'If something happens, just roll off.' But we always made it."

One day, neither Rogers nor John Orndoff was available to bring Nichols down the mountain. So four patrol members volunteered their services. Nichols laughed when he recalled that event. "While they were getting the toboggan ready… I think every one of them fell…I thought…Hey! No way am I going to ride with those characters. I skied down by myself."

Eager skiers are pulled up a jeep road on a rope attached to a snow cat.

"Los Alamos came to be known as the 'big shoulder area,'" said Bill Jarmie. "People had massive arms and shoulders from hanging on to those incredibly difficult rope tows."

Nichols considered his job of operating tow No. 3 as a "postman's holiday." Still, there were ongoing duties such as splicing torn rope and maintaining the equipment. The job of splicing wet, heavy rope was tedious, but repairing mechanical failure on the tows, in the middle of winter, was brutal.

Rogers said that two major breakdowns occurred during one ski season. A bearing on the bull wheel at tow No. 3 froze, and the engine at tow No. 1 blew.

"When the bearing froze, we took the bull wheel out and put in a small wheel that we tied to a big tree so the tow could run. We got the bull wheel down and reworked the bearing," said Rogers.

To install the repaired bull wheel, they loaded it onto a toboggan and pulled it up the mountain, but they came up short of their destination by about 20 feet.

"From there, we just manhandled it on up," Rogers said. "Then with my climbers on, I climbed the tree and remounted the bull wheel. My ears froze and were crusted for the rest of the season. In those days, I never wore a hat."

When the engine "blew" at tow No. 1, it was replaced by a Chevy V-8 engine that cost $655 dollars. Rogers said, "We took it to the shops and had a new spline made to connect to the drive wheels. Then we loaded it on a big, flat-bed truck with four-wheel drive."

It took strong backs and steely determination to install the repaired engine. Don Parker said, "There were a whole bunch of us, and John was driving this government vehicle up the mountain in a raging snowstorm." Parker said that it seemed unbelievable that the situation could become more complicated, but it did when Rogers broke a pin on the front drive shaft of the government vehicle.

"We got the truck back on the road," Rogers said. "Then we put the motor on a toboggan, and literally, ten of us pulled it up to the rope tow shed."

Parker said, "Some pushed, some pulled. We got it unloaded, moved into the shed, and positioned. Then most of us went home. The guys who knew about how the ropes worked stayed. Bob Douglas was there most of the night hooking up the safety wire system." A small crew finished the job at about two in the morning, just in time for the lift to open at 9 a.m. for weekend skiers.

The rope tows functioned as a quick and inexpensive method for hauling people to the top of the mountain, even if they seemed archaic and awkward to manage.

"Los Alamos came to be known as the 'big shoulder area,'" said Bill Jarmie. "People had massive arms and shoulders from hanging on to those incredibly difficult rope tows."

Recognition

The Los Alamos Ski Club received recognition in the January 1960 issue of *Southwestern Skier* magazine. Featured as the "Club of the Month," it was praised as "the most industrious ski club in the southwest when it comes to building their own ski area."

The article concluded, "The *Southwestern Skier* salutes the skiers of the Los Alamos Ski Club, who wanted a ski area badly enough to go out and build their own."

The Pajarito Ski Area was also featured in the February issue of *Southwestern Skier* in an article titled, "The Annual Report from Pajarito Mountain." The article noted an increase in the membership due to the increased slope and tow facilities. It praised the ski school operated by Tony and Inga Perry as being a "smashing success…their skill and popularity have made a success of professional ski instruction which had not been available at Pajarito Mountain."

Tony and Inga Perry started the ski school in 1958. The instuctors shown, from left to right are Dick Lewis, Duane Roehling, Don Parker, and Igna and Tony Perry.

In the same article, with a side title, "Who's Who At Pajarito Mountain," the article recognized seven outstanding volunteers: Bob Douglas, John Rogers, Luther Rickerson, Wes Nichols, Bob Thorn, Carl Buckland, and Mal Wallis.

Blueprint for Pajarito

A comprehensive plan for cutting slopes was approved by the Los Alamos Ski Club in the spring of 1960. Since the ski club assumed it would eventually install either a Poma or T-bar lift, the plan addressed the development of future slopes in relation to a lift path that had already been marked. The plan was divided into two phases.

Phase 1 determined the development of slopes west of the beginners area and the lodge. Lumberyard and all slopes farther west would terminate at the bottom of the proposed lift.

At the bottom of Lumberyard, a new trail would cut through a natural clearing leading to the lift. The Aspen Slope would be doubled in width and extended another 600 feet to the east summit of Pajarito Mountain.

A slope cut through a gully would lead to Two Fingers. Even when insufficient snow covered the rocks on Two Fingers, that slope would help skiers take advantage of a large, cleared area, suitable for bowl skiing. Selective rocks on Two Fingers would be blasted. The name of Two Fingers would change to Three Fingers.

During those first few years, according to Bob Thorn, the priority was to get to the top of the mountain. Lumberyard was cut to the top of the mountain, and Aspen Slope was laid out largely because the aspen trees were a lot easier to cut down than the big fir trees. "We were looking for the easiest cutting we could get done," said Thorn. "In fact, that criteria dominated the first years of cutting."

It wasn't until about 1960, when McCulloch came out with new, lightweight saws that were more dependable than the big, two-man saws that the "real slope cutting began," said Stretch Fretwell. "One person, with a good one-man saw, could do four times as much work as two of us could do with that two-man saw," said Thorn.

Senior ski racers Dale Holm, Vern Streuburg, John Jackson, and Mal Wallis stand behind young racer Pete Wallis.

Phase 2 recognized the great potential for future ski trails, yet it only addressed the expansion of Racing Slope, which would be widened and extended down through the Spring Pitch Slope to the bottom of the mountain.

Racing Slope had been proposed by Mal Wallis, an avid skier, racer, and organizer of junior races.

John Orndoff said, "When we moved to Pajarito Mountain, the junior ski racing began in earnest and the senior ski racers faded. We had no coaches except for parents. Les Seeley and Mal Wallis were probably the most knowledgeable in regard to racing technique."

Orndoff said that there was a limited area for skiing in the early days, so the Racing Club requested permission to cut a slope to be used by racers for practice. The slope would be opened for general skiing after racing practice was over.

For many years Racing Slope, a narrow run just east of Lumberyard, was where the racers ran gates and improved their technique. After Mal Wallis died in 1981, the slope was renamed in his memory. "That slope is now called Mal's Run. We cut that slope in the summers of 1961 and 1962. The chief workers were Seeley, Wallis, Tom Putnam, Orndoff, and their kids," said Orndoff.

By 1962 the ski club faced "its most critical year of need for manpower." In addition to Phases 1 and 2, three urgent projects were in progress: construction of a new lodge, installation of the power line for the T-bar, and continued slope maintenance.

An urgent call for help went out to the ski club membership. Needed were cutters, buckers, stackers, burners, blasters, rock rollers, and carpenters with simple skills.

The Second Ski Lodge

The Gamma 2 building, which served as the first ski lodge at Pajarito Mountain, was loaned temporarily from the government and eventually would be returned. When John Rogers submitted a proposal to the ski club to build a new lodge, the vote was "aye."

"I volunteered to get the design done," said Rogers. Bob Henning, an engineer at the Lab, caculated what sizes of timbers to use for the structure. William Eberhart worked on the roof rafters to determine the snow load and also worked on the floor joists. Eberhart never skied but did the work.

Stretch Fretwell, then ski club president, added that the only significant change in the design was to increase the pitch of the roof. "We put a gable on it so the snow would slide off," he said.

The budget for materials was $6,600. Volunteer labor would build the lodge. The design called for a fully insulated building with a 2,000-square-foot main room overlooking the Beginner's Slope. A ski rental shop, the ski patrol headquarters, and a coffee shop would occupy 600 square feet in the basement. A stairway would lead to an east-side entrance. Outside, a 10- by 50-foot concrete slab would serve as a sun deck.

By July 1961, the building site had been cleared, timber had been cut and burned by volunteers, the land had been bulldozed by a contractor, and the holes for the piers had been dug by the Zia Company. Prefabricated forms, made in Carl Buckland's backyard with the help of a crew of carpenters, were placed in the holes and filled in by the Los Alamos Transit-Mix Company.

"I took the forms up there on my pickup truck. Bob Jeffries, Gordon Smith, Dave Esch, and other people helped. Rainy weather nearly caused a costly delay," Buckland said. "The concrete truck came and immediately got stuck. We thought the driver would have to dump the whole load. There was a lot of concrete, because we had a form set-up for this big pad the length of the lodge. We tore out an old snow fence so the truck could back up and dump the load."

The "real work" on the lodge began in September.

"That lodge was a masterpiece of planning," said J.O. Johnson.

"The concrete truck came and immediately got stuck. We thought the driver would have to dump the whole load. There was a lot of concrete, because we had a form set-up for this big pad the length of the lodge. We tore out an old snow fence so the truck could back up and dump the load."

"John figured out every stick of lumber. He didn't waste a single piece of wood. He had it all designed and ordered. Then he had every step on the assembly planned in advance. It really went up in record time. A lot of the lumber he ordered in the right length so it didn't have to be cut or anything."

Rogers said, "We had quality wood in there...west coast fir...and vertical-grain pine wood on the floor in the main room."

Rogers had a difficult time transporting the lumber to Los Alamos. The lumber sat in a box car in Santa Fe for a couple of weeks. At last, a deal was struck with the Houston Lumber Company to provide trucks and drivers to haul the lumber to the mountain.

"For some reason, they were slow to complete the job," said Rogers. "I was impatient, so several of us went down on a Sunday to unload the lumber from the side car onto the Houston trucks. We unloaded it pretty quick. I remember the guy from the Houston Lumber Company saying, "My God! I didn't know Ph.D.'s could work like that!"

The first truckload of lumber arrived on September 30. By October 8, the framing of the lodge had progressed to the roof joists.

Rogers said, "We had a tremendous amount of help."

As chief carpenter for the lodge, Buckland knew the job would require many hundreds of man-hours to construct the building. But in a ski club newsletter, he cautioned prospective volunteers: "As lumber has been carefully planned and counted, 'spur of the moment' volunteers are not usually needed, since cutting the wrong board cannot be tolerated, in the initial framing." He urged volunteers to contact him in advance if they wished to help.

In a race against winter storms, Rogers, Buckland, and workers, along with "Lady Luck," managed to enclose the lodge with plywood sheathing, tar paper, and windows just before an 8-inch snowfall enveloped the mountain, halting further work until spring.

"Carl Buckland and I spent every Saturday, Sunday, and holiday working on the lodge until it was finished," said Rogers.

A light, powered by the generator at tow No. 2, was rigged high in the aspen trees for night work. The electrical work for the lodge was done by Roy Hopwood. As for power tools, Rogers and Buckland shared a circular saw. When they needed scaffolding for work on the outside of the lodge, they borrowed it from the Zia Company. The scaffolding would be left on a back dock so that on Saturday morning Buckland could load it in his pickup truck.

"We'd keep it until late Sunday night," said Rogers.

The days were long for Rogers and Buckland, often ending near midnight.

"I never saw such a dedicated guy as Carl," said Rogers. "It was amazing to me. If I got to the mountain at 6:30 a.m., Carl was there working."

The Cafeteria

The make-shift cafe, operated by the Explorer's Post 20 during ski racing days, moved inside the new lodge in 1962. It was first located downstairs in the northwest corner of the building, but space was tight, and only two people could work in it. "At that time, we hired a competent high school senior who did most of the ordering and cooking," said Stretch Fretwell. "He couldn't be a skier because he might sneak off and ski."

The space was inadequate, and the stairs leading to the main floor were tricky to manuever, since the top stair was about two inches higher than the others. "People would go up those stairs in good cadence, balancing a hamburger and bowl of Dan Jones' chili in each hand," said Fretwell. "Then they'd trip on the higher stair, spilling chili everywhere."

Eventually, the stairs were eliminated, and the cafe was installed on the main floor along the west wall of the lodge. The Explorer's Post provided the labor and the ski club provided the lumber. Later, the final expansion of the cafe was across the north side of the building with a small addition outside.

When the cafe expanded to the main floor, a fully paid adult was hired to oversee the total operation of the cafe. The job included ordering food and supplies, transporting all the goods and material needed for the cafe, cooking, accounting for the money at the end of the day, and training the volunteer teens from the Explorer's Post, who earned green points. The points were given a dollar value and could be spent on Post 20 trips, equipment needed for the trips, or education such as trade schools or college.

Julia Gehre, with a four-wheel-drive pick-up truck, was hired. "Julia was the gal who did it for the greatest number of years," said Fretwell. "The Explorer's Post appreciated her very much."

Weekend mornings, Julia's day began at 6 a.m. By 6:30 a.m., she was on the road, her truck loaded with all the necessities to operate the cafe, including fresh donuts and the most valuable commodity—100 gallons of water. The water was used for drinking, coffee, handwashing, and dishwashing. Gehre said, "The help used a basin in which to wash their hands. Dishwashing was kept to a minimum."

"The kitchen sink went straight into a bucket," said Fretwell. "The dish water had to be carried out and tactfully dispersed. It was not to be put into the outhouse because there was enough stuff already there to fill them up."

Gehre said, "The newly hired kids—called 'greenies'—emptied the slop buckets."

Although the cafe quarters were cramped, and breaker switches often went out because the grill and several pots were plugged into the system, Gehre said, "The kids were motivated. They were wonderful kids, great kids."

Gehre worked long hours at the ski hill, often alone until late Sunday evening. She had to count, consolidate, and pack the inventory, but there were compensations. She enjoyed working with the young people. Sometimes she'd catch a glimpse of a flock of wild turkeys or spot a deer. After a fresh snowstorm, the morning drive to the ski hill "was breathtakingly beautiful," said Gehre.

By July 5, 1962, Rogers sent a letter to the Los Alamos Ski Club Board of Directors stating:

The new ski lodge before the addition of a sun deck.

"Carl Buckland and I have nearly completed the construction of the ski lodge and by this letter are informing you of our dropping this activity."

The letter continued to outline several items that remained to be done and thanked all those people who had helped to build the lodge.

By August 1962, the lodge was finished. Buckland had planned to paint the building barn red with paint bought at a good price. "But John Rogers had a fit," he said.

Buckland said that instead the building was painted green. "The paint was green…a sick green…pale green… John and I were painting when it was raining, but there was enough overhang so we could get away with it," said Buckland.

The last chore Rogers performed was to put a wood preservative containing aromatic hydrocarbons on the vertical grain of the main floor. Then he locked the doors and went home. It was weeks before he returned to open the building.

"The vapors were appalling," he said. "If someone had lit a match in there, it would have blown-up. There were dead moths all over the place. I don't know how they got in, but they died from those fumes."

A final note from Rogers to Buckland read, "At last B. Bernard has straightened out his books, and the lodge, as you and I left it, cost $8,031.67."

Fireplace

According to J.O. Johnson, "Everybody insisted we had to have a fireplace. Couldn't have a stove; had to have a fireplace, a big circular fireplace."

Larry Madsen said that Bob Jeffries and Gordon Smith wanted to get a completely round fireplace. "They weren't cheap, and the ski club didn't have much money."

"Bob Jeffries volunteered to take care of the fireplace," said Johnson. "He wrote to several outfits. Talked to them all. Cried on their shoulder about how poor we were. We were a non-profit outfit with no money at all. Would they be willing to send us some specifications or drawings for the things, and we'd build it ourselves. One of them did."

The design advice came from Condon-King, a company in Seattle, Washington, that manufactured fireplaces. Capital Welding, in Santa Fe, agreed to fabricate the cone, which was six feet in diameter. The bowl for the fireplace came from a steel pressure vessel.

Johnson said, "When the fireplace showed up, the darn thing wouldn't fit in the door. No way we could get it in…either part—the bottom bowl or the cone—just wouldn't go in the door."

According to Johnson, Thorn and his mountain crew, who just happened to be there, solved the dilemma. "With their chain saws they quickly sawed an opening for us. That is how we got the door on the side of the lodge. With the fireplace inside, Jeffries and his crew spent much of the fall installing it," said Johnson.

To celebrate the new lodge and the fireplace, the ski club decided to have a big party. Two kegs of beer, plus plenty of food, were brought in. At dusk, on a bitterly cold night, the fireplace was inaugurated with a roaring fire. But the fireplace wouldn't draw. Smoke filled the lodge and drove the people, choking and gasping, into the frigid night.

Johnson said, "People would get a beer and stand out in the cold for as long as they could stand it. Then they'd run back inside to huddle by the fire, holding their breath while they got warm."

"People would get a beer and stand out in the cold for as long as they could stand it. Then they'd run back inside to huddle by the fire, holding their breath while they got warm."

To solve the faulty design problem, Jeffries installed a fan in the chimney. "It worked pretty good," said Johnson. "But sometimes the fan would quit, creating smoky days in the lodge."

Madsen said, "You had to bend way down below the smoke line to see all the people in the lodge. And it burned a lot of wood—a cord and a half of wood a day. It also burned forgotten gloves and boots put there by kids. The plastic would start to melt and smell."

"It was a long time before we really gave up on the fireplace and put in the electric heaters," said Johnson.

In fact, under Madsen's tenure as ski club president, 1973–74, the fireplace was removed.

The T-Bar

Plans for a mechanical ski lift had been incorporated into the initial slope planning of the ski area at Pajarito Mountain. By the summer of 1961, crews had cut a line-of-sight for the lift path and had completed a preliminary compass-survey. Cass Slocomb, of Black & Veatch, provided the club with a free professional profile survey of the lift path.

Members of the lift committee, Stretch Fretwell, Dean Taylor, and Bob Thorn, had traveled to several ski areas to investigate the various types of surface lifts.

"At that time, lift technology was such that a surface lift seemed the most practical, the safest, and the cheapest," said Ron Strong.

"Safety was a chief criteria," said Fretwell, chairman of the lift committee. A tragic incident involving a derailed Poma platter pull had occurred at one major ski area in Colorado. "Because the cable fell to the ground, when the platter derailed, it cut off a girl's leg…just sawed her leg clean off," Fretwell said.

A bulldozer pulls a truck loaded with cement up a jeep road to pour bases for the T-bar towers.

He added that if a T-bar derailed from any one tower, the design criteria required that the cable could not reach the ground. Also, the T-bar met the American National Standards Institute Aerial Tram Code (B77) for ski lifts. In fact, according to Fretwell, the New Mexico legislature later voted to require New Mexico to comply with the national standards at the urging of the Los Alamos Ski Club. Not only did the T-bar meet the criteria for safety, it presented minimal maintenance problems.

In a proposal to the ski club board, the lift committee outlined the benefits of the T-bar and suggested a method by which to pay for it. The proposal stated that the T-bar had the capacity to carry 800 skiers per hour to the top of the mountain and, ultimately, by adding additional tees, 940 skiers per hour could ride the T-bar. Other benefits listed were "ease of loading, ease of riding, one ride to the top, elimination of rope damage to clothing, low maintenance expense, virtual elimination of the all-too-familiar daily loss of skiing due to breakdown, greater participation of the members in the fun of skiing the whole of our really fine hill, and not remaining 'grounded' at the bottom."

"Since the ski club had no money and no standing at the bank," said Fretwell, "the lift committee proposed that the T-bar, estimated to cost $60,000, be financed by 10-year revenue bonds to be purchased by the ski club members." This meant that members could purchase their memberships ten years in advance.

But a voice of opposition was expressed to ski club members in a memo (Spring 1962) written by the Rope Tow Committee. The memo stated that, because of the interest paid on the bonds, the real cost of the T-bar lift would be $83,250. Acquiring a new lift would increase a membership fee to $30 ($75 per family), whereas the three rope tows could be operated with a membership fee of $8.65 ($21.64 per family).

"When it came time to replace the rope tows with commercial lifts, a vocal group wanted to stick with rope tows in order to keep Pajarito Mountain from becoming popular with outsiders," said Orndoff.

Rene Prestwood said, "The attitude to keep people out seemed to be more from the people who did not work on the mountain."

"I don't know where it came from, but it has always been a part of Los Alamos." said Thorn. "They didn't want to open the gates to the town. They never wanted people from the outside to be here, but I said, 'Boy! What I enjoy is what the rest of the world enjoys, and that's not going to keep people away from the mountain.'"

Orndoff said, "Thorn was always for progress."

In February 1962, ballots were sent to 368 adult season-ticket holders who would determine the future of the T-bar. A "yes" vote for the lift did not commit the voter to the bond issue.

At a meeting on May 22, 1962, the Los Alamos Ski Club Board of Directors felt there was sufficient support for the T-bar that they unanimously agreed to proceed with the T-bar project. The Tow Lift Committee became the "Major Lift" Committee, and the plans to install a T-bar, purchased from Hall Ski Lift Company, went into effect. In order to curb the cost of the T-bar, volunteers once again put their backs to the grind, clearing the right of way, surveying, drawing up plans, and digging holes.

Looking down Aspen Slope as cement is poured into foundations for the T-bar lift towers.

"When the T-bar was built, there was an implication far beyond just putting in the T-bar," said Thorn. "The ski club put in the electricity."

"The power line had to run from the top of West Jemez Road to the ski area," said Ron Strong. "Without the power line, the T-bar would have been impractical."

"That's when we started working Tuesday and Thursday nights," said Thorn. "...getting the wood out of the way for the power line."

Gordon (Kilowatt) Smith surveyed most of the line by himself and was largely responsible for rounding up people to dig the holes for the poles. "There was even a sign at the bottom of the mountain that read, THE GORDON SMITH REA PROJECT," said Thorn.

Strong added, "Smith was the 'chief honcho' on the project, along with Gene Tate, B.B. Fisher, Fretwell, and many others."

Orndoff said, "Digging the holes was no snap since the mountain was mostly rock."

"It was a major effort then," said J.O. Johnson. "We managed to borrow from the Zia Company a compressor and jack hammer. Then the big boys—Thorn, Harry Flaugh, and others—would jackhammer the holes. Gordon and I followed behind with the dynamite, and we'd blow these huge holes in the ground. We had to blast every hole. Then people formed work parties of two and three to dig out the holes."

The proposal stated that the T-bar had the capacity to carry 800 skiers per hour to the top of the mountain and, ultimately, by adding additional tees, 940 skiers per hour could ride the T-bar.

"It was difficult to maneuver the big, long shovels that linemen used to dig holes eight feet deep. You stood on top of them," said Thorn.

"I remember when it was raining, really raining, and Don Parker and I were virtually digging that hole by hand," said Prestwood. "The water was coming in faster than the dirt was going out."

"I remember when it was raining, really raining, and Don Parker and I were virtually digging that hole by hand," said Prestwood. "The water was coming in faster than the dirt was going out."

Prestwood said that they had a coffee can and, since he was the smallest person they could find, he went headfirst down into the hole to bail out the water.

"I'm holding onto his feet while he dips the can, lifts it up and I'd grab it," said Parker. "This was not a normal operation."

"I doubt we dug more than a couple of feet in a matter of a couple of hours, during that driving rain storm, to put in a dumb telephone pole," said Prestwood. "How dumb can you be?"

Professional labor completed the T-bar project.

The Robert E. McKee Company, contractor to the Laboratory, was hired, at a cost of $18,690, to set about 70 power poles, pour the concrete for the T-bar towers and terminals, and to erect 20 towers, which would support the cables for the lift.

Strong said, "They were shamed and coerced into taking the installation contract. No profit was made on the installation."

The construction crew faced a tough problem, according to an article in the October 12, 1962, issue of *LASL News*. In order to set the footings for the towers, they had to figure out how to haul tons of ready-mixed concrete up the steep slopes of Pajarito Mountain.

The devised plan was three-fold. On the lower portion of the lift path, a ready-mix concrete truck was pushed up the slope by a bulldozer. Then a bulldozer pulled a dump truck, loaded with heavy, ready-mixed concrete to the upper part of the mountain. On the middle portion of the lift path, a caterpillar tractor carried the wet concrete to the footings in a bucket mounted on its front. So by pushing and pulling and tugging and straining and sweating, the men completed the job.

The power line that fed the electrical motors that ran the ski lift stretched over a four-mile route. It was installed by the Reynolds Electric Company, which donated many insulators and poles. However, most of the power poles, which came from the Laboratory's old Technical 1 area, were retrieved from Zia salvage. The AEC provided terminal switchgear and transformers. The ski club spent about $5,000 for power line materials.

In October 1962, a ski club newsletter recognized B.B. Fisher, Thorn, and others for doing "a tremendous job of clearing the power line right-of-way, the T-bar line, and increasing the down hill room on the Aspen Slope."

Gordon Smith thanked "all those people who had worked so hard to complete the club's project."

But work on the mountain was never done. Once the T-bar was installed, every season the tees had to be attached to the bars and removed in the spring.

"The first time, we didn't know what we were doing," said Bob Rohwer. "The cable was so high we had to have scaffolding for people to stand on."

Johnson said, "The scaffolding, with a platform on top where people stood, was gerry rigged from old lumber we had gotten from the high school stadium bleachers."

Prestwood said, "The way it worked, a tee was put onto the cable, and what we called 'hot dogs,' made of rubber, were put on either side of the tee, which fixed the tees on the cable. With the 'hot dogs' on either side of the tee, when it went over the rollers, it wouldn't chew up the rollers. So we could get those 'hot dogs' on, we'd boil them in hot water, which made them very pliable. I was boiling, and others were on the scaffolding, putting up the tees. Suddenly, a tee caught the scaffolding and dragged timbers uphill."

Ivar Lindstrom recalled that he was standing on the southeast corner of the scaffolding when it collapsed beneath him.

"Ivar grabbed the cable and rode through the first set of pulleys," said Rohwer. "We were screaming at him, "Let Go! Let Go!" Lindstrom dropped to the ground unharmed. "He was the very first person to ride the T-bar," laughed Johnson.

"There wasn't much tension on the cable," Lindstrom said. "I had on gloves, so it didn't hurt."

Teenagers Kyle Thorn and Kay Rohwer ride the T-bar over visible grass, dirt, and stumps in the path.

Rohwer, Taylor, Wallis, and Ed Grilly returned one Sunday to finish installing the tees. Late that afternoon, Rohwer and Taylor rode the T-bar to the top of the mountain. Thus, they were the first people to ride the T-bar.

As he skied down the mountain, Rohwer "made one of my usual inept turns and fell." Grilly drove him to the hospital, where he was diagnosed with a broken back. "I spent six weeks in a cast but skied three of those weekends in a body cast. I wouldn't do that today," he added.

Ironically, Rohwer opposed the T-bar. "I thought it would get people who didn't ski worth a damn too high on top of the mountain, and they were going to get in trouble," he said.

Bill Jarmie, a ski patroller, agreed. "During the rope tow days, wonderful, experienced skiers made it to the top. There were few accidents on top of the mountain. When the T-bar came in, people started getting hurt," said Jarmie.

In a 1962 ski club newsletter, skiers were cautioned not to ride the T-bar to the top of the mountain if they could not do a stem christie. The newsletter also listed procedures for loading, unloading, and reloading the T-bar, which was permitted only at the bottom terminal or the intermediate landing.

Strong said, "Part of the sales pitch for the lift was the inclusion of an intermediate unloading station. This would allow beginners to use the lower part of Aspen, an easy slope. This feature was less than successful."

Riding the T-bar was as tricky as riding the rope tows. Choosing a riding partner, preferably of similar size, was important. "Kids were always looking for someone to go up with. Some of them couldn't hold the tee down," said Strong. "They always picked tall men. That way the kids could have the tee under their rear ends, which is about knee high for the man."

During years when snow was plentiful, keeping the T-bar path clear was a challenge.

Harry Flaugh said, "In a bad snow year, the T-bar would pick up a kid or even a small adult. In other years, with a lot of snow, the tees would drag, making little stair steps." To solve the problem, local youth were hired to shovel the tow path.

"These were grim reapers of kids," said Strong. "The shovelers would sit and slide on the shovel between the places requiring maintenance. This was how we started the shovel races at Skiesta."

Flaugh said, "One Skiesta, I ran the shovel race. I thought I could ski down the mountain pretty fast, but one of the shovelers beat me down the mountain, faster than I could ski."

In 1965, the shovelers were replaced by a bulldozer that was used to cut a swath down the T-bar path. Wendell Seitz was the only person to run that bulldozer down the T-bar path. Volunteers pulled the tees aside so the dozer could get by.

"We'd ride up on the bulldozer. Then we'd ski down and hold the tees out to one side so the dozer could go down," said Johnson. "Then we'd ski the powder down to the next tees and do the same. We'd get in a little bit of powder skiing." But the bulldozer wasn't perfect, as it dug a trench three to four feet deep.

"If you fell off, you were in trouble," said Johnson.

"If someone fell and was sliding down the trench, with no way out, someone would scream! So, the first person near a tower would slap a red safety button that was on each tower. The tee would shut down."

Herman Rohr, who operated the T-bar, would use binoculars to scan the mountain, watching for people to wave at him, signaling that it was safe to restart the lift.

"He never restarted the tow until it was safe," said Rohwer.

This method was not fool proof. Flaugh said that he and George Hill witnessed an accident that involved a little girl who fell off the tee and slid face first down the T-bar path. "The people on the tee behind the little girl didn't know that they needed to bail off the tee.

The tip of a ski hit the girl in the face and tore her cheek, which was all bloody.... We didn't know much first aid, so we just put a handkerchief over it." said Flaugh.

"Now I understand why the insurance company recommended we get rid of the T-bar," said Bob Kirby, a past president of the ski club.

Future for the Ski Area

John Orndoff unloads at the top of the mountain.

By September 1963, the initial comprehensive plan, Phases 1 and 2, had been completed.

In fact, Gordon Smith, ski club president for the year 1963–64, felt pretty good about the situation on Pajarito Mountain. In a newsletter, October 18, 1963, he wrote:

"I was just sitting here in my rocking chair congratulating myself on having been so astute as to have chosen this year to serve as your president. The ski hill is in such fine shape, at least compared to this time last year, that it is amazing. As far as I can see from this comfortable position my biggest problem is that I can't get Joyce to peel me any grapes.

"However I would not want you to believe that this all came about without considerable effort so I will try to enumerate the various tasks that have been completed this summer. I have intentionally not mentioned any names for two reasons, (1) I would be unable to give proper credit where it is due, (2) those who are interested in knowing to whom they are indebted for our ski area already know the names."

In that same newsletter, Smith said that a new slope (Wildcat) had been cut, cleared, and burned. He added that an organized attack had been made on aspen shoots and, on October 5 and 6, some 35 people were active with all sorts of tools attacking those shoots. Also, a motor-driven weed cutter, purchased by the club, seemed to work well for those souls hardy enough to handle it. He wrote, "The results are quite rewarding, in that the slopes are nearly free of the little monsters."

He was also pleased to report that all the pulleys on the rope tow had been rejuvenated and had grease fittings installed in them. It was planned to have an electric heater in the engine to facilitate starting it, and a new rope had been ordered. Also, the electrical system on the T-bar had been improved. Plus, the membership would be pleased to know that the new powder rooms (the outhouses) were under construction and would be completed in time for the ski season. Once again, a call for help ended the newsletter. "There will be work parties on the hill every weekend until snow."

"The shovelers would sit and slide on the shovel between the places requiring maintenance. This was how we started the shovel races at Skiesta."

To encourage volunteerism as a family project, one newsletter stated: "Here is something that we can all do—women and children to haul the slash, the men to handle the logs." So the volunteers settled into the summer routine of building a ski area on Pajarito Mountain.

Don Parker said that the new outhouses replaced the two single holers, which were originally installed near the old lodge.

"Jim Bridge and I dug the holes for the outhouses," said Parker. "We poured all four slabs in my back yard. Then we hauled them up in Jim's truck and carried them over to the site in a wheelbarrow. We laid down the slabs, then cemented them in."

By the late sixties, several slopes extend from top to bottom, and a line has been cut for a chair lift on the east side of the mountain.

After that job was completed, Parker said, "Jim took off, saying he was through. The rest of that summer, I worked on the top part. People would come by and donate an hour or so. Gene Tate helped paint the brown trim."

"Eventually, we workers tended to specialize," said Orndoff. "I ended up installing most of the pulleys on trees for the rope tows. And in the fall, Mal Wallis and I used to cut aspen shoots, using the motorized brush cutters."

Specialties would change over time, but during those early years, Orndoff said, "John Rogers was the chief rope splicer, and he had lots of work. Tom Putnam's specialty was communications for the Ski Patrol. Rene Prestwood's specialty was burning slash. Bob Thorn was the chief tree cutter."

By 1965, it had become clear to the ski club that skiing had become popular with the locals and people throughout the country.

In fact, according to a memo dated April 1965, "The popularity and growth of Pajarito Mountain has probably exceeded the expectations of any of the early planners," and "the current healthy condition of the club is due to the hard work and interest of many volunteers and if the programs outlined by the Planning Committee are to be carried out even more help is needed."

When the T-bar was installed, the current facilities seemed adequate. However, the Planning Committee concluded that, as the ski area became more attractive, it would continue to draw more members and outsiders to the mountain.

Incredibly, in such a short time, the ski club found that the parking was inadequate. The lodge was overcrowded. As growth continued, the lifts and slopes would be inadequate. So, if the ski club were to adhere to its objective of providing pleasant skiing, with no lines or overcrowded slopes, it must expand. Thus, in the same memo, the

Planning Committee suggested an ambitious plan for expansion of the ski area.

In retrospect, the most forward recommendation was to acquire more land, which made sense if the ski club were to develop more slopes and install more lifts. The Planning Committee urged the club to acquire land to the east from the AEC and to purchase land to the west owned by the Baca family. It was also suggested that the club be prepared to buy the land that it was currently leasing within a two-year period. Assuming that the ski club would acquire additional land to the east and west, the Planning Committee outlined a plan for developing the slopes.

The memo stated that the current slopes were centered on ski club land. It described the area to the east as north facing and covered with aspen trees. It recommended that wide slopes over gentle terrain could be cut to provide advanced beginning to intermediate skiing. It also stated that the east area would be the easiest to develop for the needs of the majority of skiers. Looking to the future, the committee foresaw that the east area, which extended eastward from Racing Slope (the lower part was called Baby Doe), would be served by a new lift (east lift). The committee recommended that Daisy Mae be continued to the bottom and that other intermediate slopes be cut in anticipation of an early east lift installation. Meanwhile, skiers using the east area could return to the T-bar by traversing above the beginner's slopes or by using the beginner's rope tow and then traversing over.

"Jim Bridge and I dug the holes for the outhouses," said Parker. "We poured all four slabs in my back yard. Then we hauled them up in Jim's truck and carried them over to the site in a wheelbarrow."

The area to the west had a greater vertical drop over steeper, more interesting terrain. However, it faced northeast and received more sun. Slopes would have to be narrow so that they could be shaded by the large fir and spruce trees. These narrow, steep slopes would be more difficult to clear; however, this type of terrain provided an excellent challenge for the more advanced or expert skier. The committee strongly recommended that the ski club acquire the West Peak, either by purchase, lease, or use permit.

A 1965 memo described the west area as extending from Racing Slope westward to the county line and served by a T-bar (the west lift). It had two high-traffic slopes, Aspen and Lumberyard; one medium-traffic slope, Racing Slope / Baby Doe; and one low-traffic slope, Wildcat. In addition, the Two Fingers region was used moderately when snow conditions were good.

The committee recommended that Wildcat be widened to increase its use. It suggested that a slope be cut down the gully into Two Fingers, with a traverse back to Wildcat, and that the remainder of the area above Two Fingers, west of Wildcat, be reserved for park or glade skiing. The latter proposal would involve thinning out the smaller trees and removing the dead fall.

Rope tows No. 1 and 2 still served the beginner's area, which separated the east and west slopes at the bottom of the mountain. The memo noted that the slope above the lodge, served by rope tow No. 2, was the only one used extensively and that the area east of rope tow No. 1 (The Meadow) was little used. The Meadow slope, if extensively cleared, would provide increased capacity for beginning skiers. The committee proposed that a lower landing be put on the No. 2 rope tow and that the top landing on rope tow No. 1 be improved.

The memo also recommended that future lift lines be positioned now so that future slopes would not cross lift paths. It further recommended that the lift line on the east side should be established near the Daisy Mae slope. The committee also suggested that a line of sight should be cut and a survey made so that the club would be in a position to install the lift when a $30,000 annual income was reasonably certain.

A crew surveys a line for a chair lift on the east side.

Should the West Pajarito Peak become available, the committee thought that the area could be serviced by installing a lift, such as a rope tow, from the saddle to the peak to be used in conjunction with the present T-bar. As for the beginner's area, the committee believed that the two rope tows, which were relatively trouble free and accommodated about 1,000 skiers per hour, seemed to be adequate for the foreseeable future.

The Planning Committee also felt that the parking situation, the lodge, and slope maintenance needed immediate attention.

Parking on peak skiing days had become a nightmare. The Camp May Road, owned by the county, was so narrow in front of the lodge that when cars parked parallel on both sides, traffic could barely negotiate, creating a one-way lane. The lower parking area, on land that belonged to the AEC, allowed some diagonal parking on one side and parallel parking on the other side. The county road to the east was not wide enough to allow parking with a two-way traffic pattern. So the committee recommended a one-way loop going west. This configuration used the county road and the lower parking lot and was the cheapest and easiest to control.

The lodge, just three years old, needed renovation to allow for more rental space, cafeteria space, and seating area. It was recommended that a sun deck be installed in front of the building with benches and tables to be provided. Ski racks would be installed outside of the sun deck. The cafeteria would be put upstairs, which would allow the rental shop to extend its operation into the vacated cafeteria space.

The last item to be addressed by the Planning Committee was slope maintenance.

In the memo, the Planning Committee reviewed the many problems associated with slope maintenance. During winter, if there was too little snow, rocks, stumps, logs, and aspen shoots showed through the snow. Conversely, too much snow formed large, steep moguls, which became progressively bigger as the season continued. The memo stated, "Moguls can be fun to ski but as a steady diet and especially after a fresh snowfall they are a nuisance."

Vehicle access to the mountain was a dilemma for people with supplies and heavy equipment. The committee suggested that more roadways be bladed out so that slopes could be cut more easily. In addition to slope cutting, shoot cutting and burning could be accomplished more efficiently if people with chain saws, burners, kerosene, weed cutters, gasoline, explosives, and packs could drive closer to the work areas. Also, should the ski club membership vote to purchase a bulldozer, the roadways would allow it to go up to the steeper parts of the the mountain.

Parking on peak skiing days had become a nightmare. The Camp May Road, owned by the county, was so narrow in front of the lodge that when cars parked parallel on both sides, traffic could barely negotiate, creating a one-way lane.

To strengthen the case for purchasing the bulldozer, the committee stressed that other areas had been very successful with winter slope maintenance by using bulldozers to control moguls and scrape snow over exposed areas. Not only could the bulldozer, equipped with blade extensions and wide tracks, scrape the tops off the moguls, it could pack the loosened snow in the troughs. In addition, it could be used to pack fresh fallen snow on the beginners area, smooth out tow paths and terminal areas, and do minor clearing in the parking lot. The committee recommended that a bulldozer, of the type used at Aspen and Vail, Colorado, be purchased that year; that a shed be built to house the dozer; and that a person be hired to operate the dozer on occasional weekdays during the skiing season. Financially, the committee said that the ski club had enough money for a sizable down payment, and the rest of the money could be borrowed from the manufacturer or bank, using the machine as collateral.

Ballots to vote on the bulldozer were distributed to the membership in June 1965, but there was opposition in the membership toward purchasing the bulldozer.

Bob Rohwer opposed buying the bulldozer. "I didn't even know the term mogul in those days. The bumps were an annoyance, but I couldn't see this dozer," he said. "I was convinced that it was going to pack the snow too hard, make it too smooth. It was going to ruin the mountain for experienced skiers." Poking fun at himself, Rohwer laughed, "Of course, I'd only been skiing for three years."

Rohwer thought the old way of breaking down the bumps was "a perfectly reasonable way to take care of the bumps." He said that there was always a shovel stuck in the top of one of the bumps, so when a person skied off he grabbed a shovel and shoveled off the top of the bump and filled in the valley below it. Then he skied down and stuck the shovel in the next bump for the next skier.

However, Margaret Flaugh said, "I hated skiing Lumberyard, because the moguls were so big. When somebody went down, you couldn't see them, so that terrified me. When I'd fall, I was always afraid that someone would come barreling down and hit me. I was all for knocking the moguls down."

Nevertheless, the opposition to the new dozer was strong.

J.O. Johnson said, "They campaigned and put out their little newsletter as to why we shouldn't buy the dozer."

Except for the 19 people who opposed the purchase of the bulldozer, the membership favored its purchase.

Dozers are used to contour slopes, create jeep roads, and control moguls.

Rohwer said, "The 19 of us that voted against the dozer got some old metal buttons, which in those days was the ski club badge, and we sprayed them gold. We wrote the number 19 on them and wore them the whole season."

Johnson said, "They proudly wore those buttons while the rest of us complained about the terrible job of packing that dozer did. They'd stand there and say, 'Well, we didn't vote for it.'"

Rohwer was very reactionary as a young man and thought everything should stay the same forever. "I fought many of the improvements on the ski hill. Turns out I was wrong at the time.

You've got to change and keep up with things. The best way to take care of change is to be part of it, so I'm going to keep on working at the ski hill."

The bulldozer bought by the ski club was a small crawler tractor with dozer blades that could move snow to bare spots, pack snow, and bust moguls. "It had an option to convert it into a groomer," said Rohwer. "Despite the fact that I voted against it, every fall, I and others jacked the thing up, took the tracks and wheels off, put axle extensions on to spread it out wider. Then we put the wheels back on to the extended axles and put wider treads back on. The traditional dozer had tracks about two feet wide. The snow tracks were two or three times as wide. We usually used it to bulldoze out the big bumps. It wasn't a snow groomer to the extent that the modern machines are today."

Milt Gillespie said, "Grooming really began with the John Deere 350."

Harry Flaugh said, "It was a mogul planer. One year we had a ski race scheduled. Lumberyard was badly moguled, so Wendell Seitz was going to mogul-plane it."

Flaugh volunteered to help Seitz, but before they finished planing the slope, two feet of snow fell on the mountain. Flaugh said, "Here is this hard, mogul-covered slope with snow over it. It was just terrifying. We had no control. We jammed the blade into a mogul, then we'd break through and jam the blade into the next mogul. I was terrified. When we got down, I told Seitz he was crazy. We can't do that. But, he wasn't ready to give up, so he went back up again. It scared me enough I wouldn't ride the darn thing. When Seitz got back down he wouldn't do it again either."

Flaugh said that the irony of the story is that, the next day, they had to groom the slope with shovels to make the race course on Lumberyard."

Gillespie had a number of horror stories about grooming. He recalled a ride down Lumberyard with Wendell Seitz that nearly took out the fourth tower on the T-bar. There was about four feet of soft snow. "The machine just oozed down the mountain. The only way you could steer it was by the angle on the blade. That was how Wendel missed the tower," said Gillespie.

Milt Gillespie operates a John Deere dozer.

There were occasions when the bulldozer plowed into a tree or rolled over. Johnson recalled the first incident with the new John Deere. "I don't believe we had it operating more than a week or two when the drive axle broke at the top of the Beginner's Slope, about where the beginner's chair terminates today. The bulldozer slid sideways and ended up by a tree."

The bulldozer was under warranty, so the John Deere dealer sent a mechanic with replacement parts to fix it. Johnson said that he, Rene Prestwood, Bob Thorn, and Gordon Smith took the day off work to help. They loaded tools and the mechanic, who couldn't ski, into toboggans, which they pulled up the mountain via the old rope tow. "It was snowing, so we built a roaring fire so people could get their hands warm. But we got it apart and put in the new axle."

He recalled a ride down Lumberyard with Wendell Seitz that nearly took out the fourth tower on the T-bar. There was about four feet of soft snow. "The machine just oozed down the mountain. The only way you could steer it was by the angle on the blade. That was how Wendel missed the tower," said Gillespie.

It wasn't uncommon for the operator of the bulldozer to walk down the mountain, get a chain saw, walk back to the bulldozer, and cut it free from a tangle of timber or a tree.

One of the most freakish accidents that one could imagine, Gillespie remembered, occurred when the bulldozer came too close to the woods. The blade on the mogul planer, which was pulled behind the bulldozer, hooked a tall, dead aspen tree. The tree snapped, and as it was pulled forward by the mogul planer, it broke over the top of the cab, pitched forward down the slope and dug into a bank like a javelin, with the sharp point sticking out of the snow toward the bulldozer. "The driver couldn't stop. The pointed end came through the windshield. It went beside his head into the back of the cab," said Gillespie.

Generally, bulldozers were considered to be quite stable and difficult to turn over. However, Larry McDowell found himself in a "scare of his life" when the dozer rolled three times. Gillespie said that they could count the number of times it had rolled, because they could see the track marks where it struck the ground. According to Gillespie, this happened before the days of a roll-over protective structure that OSHA now requires. The old lore of caterpillar drivers was to never climb out the uphill side because the caterpillar is coming at you as it rolls faster than you can possibly climb. "Larry threw himself out of the dozer on the downhill side and got out of the way as fast as he could," said Gillespie. "It scared all of us. He was bruised but not hurt. The bulldozer came to rest at a horrible angle on one track. Then the ground gave way, causing it to make one more partial roll into a tree. That was the beginning of the end for the 350."

On nice days, the sun deck provides a pleasant place for skiers to relax and enjoy the area developed by their friends and neighbors.

By October 5, 1965, a ski club newsletter reported: "Never has so much been done by so few. Thanks to the persistence of a few "hard core" club members and the efforts of several newcomers, you will find your ski area much improved."

Daisy Mae had been widened and doubled in length. Upper Wildcat had been widened. Selected trees had been removed on Lumberyard and at the top of the Beginner's Slope. Also, countless evergreen and deciduous trees had been removed from in front of the lodge. And the bulldozer had been hard at work clearing land for a new jeep road and parking lot expansion.

Renovations to the lodge, which included a decor likened to "New Normandy-Bistro" and described as "carefully and imaginatively designed to provide the ultimate in physical and psychological comfort," had been completed. The new sun deck was under construction. Gordon Smith spearheaded the project to add the sun deck to the new lodge. Always scrambling for money, the ski club kept an eye out for good deals. When Smith had learned that Los Alamos High School planned to replace the wooden bleachers at the football field, he made an offer the school couldn't resist. Thus, the deck, as well as the scaffolding for the T-bar, was built with recycled lumber from the high school bleachers at a cost of $2,000.

The sun deck became a cluttered mecca of skiers resting, eating, drinking, and socializing, even a place for local amusement at the expense of out-of-town skiers. Following a heavy snowfall, the out-of-town skiers often sat at the empty picnic tables, placed beneath the slanted portion of the roof that dipped toward the deck. Ed and Ev Griggs said that the local skiers enjoyed a "hearty chuckle when the visitors were startled by an avalanche of melting snow cascading upon them. Eventually, as a matter of safety, no tables were placed in that area after a snowfall," said the Griggs. "But we had our fun while it lasted."

Shaping the Ski Slopes

Consider the art and the danger in felling trees!

Consider the task of shaping a ski slope, covered with heavy fir, spruce, and aspen trees. Which tree comes down first? How will it fall? What tree comes down next?

Consider the chore of cutting the felled trees into manageable lengths, to be rolled into the woods or slashed, stacked, and burned!

Consider slope improvements, such as busting the tree stumps, blasting rocks, or cutting aspen shoots!

Consider cutting all the jeep trails that crisscross the mountain, which allow workers access to the slopes during the summer and provide trails back to the lodge for skiers during the winter!

Consider cutting the paths for the chair lifts, building the ramps, and the tow shacks!

Consider the lodges, from the first to the last, built by volunteer help!

The task was formidable. Over a period of 40 years, hundreds of volunteers and thousands of man-hours shaped Pajarito Mountain into a magnificent skiscape.

Bob Thorn, top, and Harry Flaugh, below, were two of the most dedicated volunteers on Pajarito Mountain, and cutting trees was their first love (besides skiing).

Bob Thorn said, "I saw something that could be developed. There was lots of room to put in lifts. It had a north-facing slope. It would have been nice if it had 600 more feet of vertical rise, in which case, I think it would have been just about right, but nevertheless, for a mountain with 1,100 to 1,200 feet of vertical rise, it has a great deal of variety to offer."

According to Stretch Fretwell, "Bob Thorn was one of the big power houses on slope planning and liked doing the felling."

"Bob Thorn and chain saws were made for each other," said J.O. Johnson.

In the early years, Thorn would put his chain saw, a gas can, a cooler with beer, and lunch into the trunk of the family sedan, a black, two-door Ford, which he drove to the top of the mountain.

Rene Prestwood remembers the black Ford. "It was our total transportation on the mountain. When we went up on the mountain, Bob and I had a cigar in our mouths, kerosene in the front seat that sat between my legs, gasoline cans behind the front seat for the chain saws, and two burners in the continental kit in the back. That's how we hit the mountain."

Though Thorn often worked on the mountain alone, a dedicated crew of men soon joined him. They worked Saturdays, Sundays, and Wednesday nights. Years later, they stopped working on Sundays.

"The mountain was a diversion," said Prestwood. "That's what we did for relaxation."

Thorn and his loggers came to be known as the "lumberjack types."

"The felling itself goes back to marking the slopes," said Larry Madsen. "So those guys were the artists. They put in the character of the slope."

Harry Flaugh added that often, when the cutters skied the trees during the ski season, they would decide which trees should be cut (the selected trees were marked with paint).

Stretch Fretwell said, "It was more than cutting that Thorn did. One had to put some cuts into the trees to make them fall on the contour."

"When we went up on the mountain, Bob and I had a cigar in our mouths, kerosene in the front seat that sat between my legs, gasoline cans behind the front seat for the chain saws, and two burners in the continental kit in the back. That's how we hit the mountain."

However, the trees often fell into each other, which caused a "tangle." This situation became especially dangerous when the trees fell into a lot of deadfall.

When the cutting is done in an area where there is a lot of deadfall, it creates a dangerous situation. "One tree goes up against another and another until there are perhaps five trees all hung up together," said Ron Strong.

"These are called widow makers," said Harry Flaugh.

According to Strong, "Very carefully, we try to plan an escape route as we go down. We hope that the next tree we cut is going to clear the whole mess. We try to get out of the way, because this tree slides this way and that one the other way."

Flaugh recalled a bad situation when he, Gene Moore, and Ron Strong had felled several trees in the lower west parking lot. "They were really a mess. It was just a tangle," said Flaugh. "You do everything you can to put the trees on the slope, but it's only of matter to time before you hang up a tree."

Flaugh was cutting up above Strong and Moore when he saw the situation unfold. "Ron was cutting one of the last of the few trees. Gene had laid his saw down to help push the tree toward where they wanted it to fall. But there were two trees standing together, and their branches had tangled up in the top. When they pushed the one tree, it spun in one direction and went down, but they didn't see that the other tree had broken off too. It came down and hit both of them. That's all I could see. I threw my saw down and ran to them as quick as I could. There was a whole matte of trees around, so when the tree came down, it smashed them onto those trees. The trees had taken off the load. Gene's helmet was broken," said Flaugh.

In another incident, when Harry's tooth was broken, Margaret, his wife, said it really scared her.

According to Harry, he wasn't paying attention while cutting some branches and hadn't noticed that a branch had hooked unto another. The branch broke loose and hit Harry in the head. "It drove my head down into my chest and shoved my lower jaw into the upper and sheered off a tooth," he said.

Margaret added that a "widow maker" almost got Jim Hedstrom.

When a log broke loose, "Jim laid down in a depression. The log rolled right over him," she said.

As trees often went in directions unintended, saws occasionally got stuck in the trees.

"When a saw hung up, you'd have to get someone with another saw. Typically, you'd cut above the stuck saw," said Flaugh. "One time Ron and I were working on a big tree when this brand new saw got stuck. We cut the tree above the saw, but it didn't fall in the right direction. It fell and hit the the brand new saw."

"I remember when there were three saws stuck in the same tree," said Bob Rohwer. "I don't know how we ever got them out."

According to Rene Prestwood, "It wasn't unusual to get a saw stuck in a tree. As you're taking the saw out, a little breeze comes by and pinches the saw in the tree. The chances of getting the saw out are practically nil."

One day Prestwood's saw got stuck. He walked up to Harry Flaugh, who was cutting a few hundred yards away from him. "I said, 'Harry, come help me. I got myself stuck.' Harry comes down to help, and there is my saw on the ground. The tree had fallen over."

No one lost fingers to the chain saws, but ironically, a chain saw broke Bob Thorn's leg. Prestwood said, "Robert had a chain saw in his hand and when he stepped back on a round twig, his foot went one way, and he went down. The chain saw went up in the air and came down, right on his leg. It wasn't running, but the impact of it broke his leg. Bob wore a full leg cast and was grouchy as hell the rest of the summer." Prestwood's log shows that the incident occurred on Saturday, June 14, 1969.

Evan Ballard takes a break from cutting.

After the trees were felled, the bucking crew came in.

"That was largely a Wednesday night project," said Madsen. "The buckers cut up the wood so it could be stacked."

"I've been up there on Wednesday when 10 or 12 chain saws were going. We'd go up at five o'clock and work until dark," said Prestwood. "I used to have my own chain saw I kept in the trunk of my car. I mean, Robert let me have my own saw so nobody else could screw it up."

Typically, the buckers often complained about the fellers, when all the trees fell into a tangle. Madsen said, "The biggest tangle I ever saw was on lower Big Mother. It was like jack straw. I fell off a log one day and fell 10 feet.

Then the stackers complained about the buckers, who may have been a bit lazy and didn't want to bend over to cut the branches off the bottom of the logs.

Then burners complained about the stackers, who didn't want to drag the slash into tight stacks, so there wasn't much but air in piles to burn. Or, in early summer, the timber was wet and difficult to burn.

Strong said, "We always complained about ourselves, that is, the fellers were also the buckers, the stackers, and the burners."

"We had to learn how to burn," said Thorn.

The initial procedure was to stack the wood in a pile, smother it in gasoline, and torch it with a match.

From top: Gene Moore cuts branches off a tree; Harry Flaugh and Ron Strong after a long day of burning.

"There would be a great big flame," said Thorn, "then, immediately, it would go out. It took a great concentration of heat to get the piles to burn, especially when the wood was green and absolutely wet."

Finally, the ski club purchased weed burners from the Sears, Roebuck and Company catalog. The weed burners could produce enough heat to burn the piles of wood.

Rene Prestwood said, "Billy Fisher was the first official head burner. We never saw Billy after he got married, so the job fell into my hands."

At first, the burners were fueled with kerosene, bought in 5-gallon containers. Condensation often occurred, and the water in the kerosene caused problems. Later, it was discovered that diesel fuel worked just as well and better.

Strong said, "The old burners were like blowtorches or Coleman stoves. You had to get the fuel in the coil hot enough to generate vapor. Toilet paper was stuffed into the coil, soaked with diesel fuel, and lit. Once one blowtorch caught fire, then it was used to start the rest. Now propane burners are used to start the fuel burners."

Today, these same old, obsolete weed burners are used. Every year, these burners have to be taken apart, cleaned, repaired, and reassembled. "The burners are temperamental," said Prestwood. "They hold three gallons of fuel."

Markeita Hedstrom said, "Stan Moore is the real ramrodder on that. He takes them home. He makes parts."

Thorn said, "I always thought we ought to have been smart enough to invent something a little better and make something a little bit sturdier, but we never did."

Before burning could occur, certain procedures had to be followed. All burning activity had to be coordinated through the local Fire Department. There were other agencies that had to be contacted such as the Espanola District Ranger, Bandelier Monument, the police department, and KRSN, the local radio station.

Prestwood held the job of head burner for about 12 years before he "passed the torch" of burning onto Larry Madsen.

"Rene groomed me," said Madsen. "He taught me how to run a burner with great patience. Then, I retired early and willed it to Markeita."

"When I inherited the job as head burner, I was handed this burn folder that said 'notes.' Inside were all those phone numbers that I had to call before we could burn," said Markeita. "Today, the area manager does the calling."

In the fall, on burn days, the people burning arrived at the mountain at about eight o'clock in the morning.

"It would be so darn cold. We'd be standing in the middle of the road, freezing to death," said Markeita.

The first year that Markeita burned, someone gave her a burner with a faulty strap. By the end of the day, her knees and legs were black and blue from the burner banging into her.

Despite that, Markeita enjoyed burning because it was something different. But she found burning very hard work until she learned how to burn.

"You'd throw the burner over your shoulder. The barrel is over your back. Then you take the wand and stick it into the pile and hope it catches fire. If you trip, you could burn to death. We burned in pairs, because sometimes the burner would go out. It was easier to have someone close by."

Burning is hot and dirty work. Top, from left: Harry Flaugh, Bob Thorn, and Rene Prestwood relax while an unidentified man's face is obscured by smoke. Jim and Markeita Hedstrom smile for the camera.

"Burning is miserable work," said Prestwood. "It is harder than using a chain saw. The heat is so bad. Through the years, I don't know how many cuffs I burned off my gloves."

"We'd usually burn up the mountain, so that the wind wasn't in our faces," said Markeita, "but one time, the fire turned and curled around me. Very scary. I was singed some."

"There were days when the wind was just in the wrong direction. You couldn't get away from it," said Madsen. "We'd light these green pine needles, and there would be this thick, white, acrid smoke. It about killed you."

"The smoke would take your breath away," said Markeita. "Years ago, I used to wear a wig by choice. So, one year, when I went to burn, I put on my wig, a scarf over my head and went up the mountain to burn. When I got home and looked into the mirror, the whole wig had melted. But, no one said a word. They were really nice."

Definitely, burning could be dangerous!

Prestwood said, "When we burned Porcupine Park, it was extremely dry, and we almost burned John Orndoff."

Bob Rohwer said, "John was in a section by himself when the fire quickly spread."

"He was surrounded by this great fire," said Prestwood.

Rohwer said, "I looked up and saw John, walking through this wall of flame."

"They thought I was trapped in between the blazes," said Orndoff. "Finally, I peered out from the smoke. I get kidded about that."

During the summer, the cutting crew cuts the trees down and bucks them in pieces small enough for stacking and burning.

Dry conditions often caused a burn to flare out of control or the fire could travel along what is called a "punky root," which is a dry, rotten root. "It acts like a wick," said Flaugh.

One such incident occurred on Big Mother. The fire had crept down beneath the tuff and smoldered. Eventually, it resurfaced and scorched many areas along the edge of Big Mother. The burn crew dubbed the charred debris, Black Bark Beetle Infestation.

Madsen said, "In the early days, before the big wood was hauled away, some of those logs burned for days."

Kyle Wheeler remembers taking many trips with her father, Bob Thorn, to check on burn piles. "I remember sleeping in the old lodge during the night when we were burning and listening to the mice running around in the dark," she said.

"I must say, that over 30 years, we never had a fire get really out of control, though we had a few marginal cases," said Prestwood. "Most of the time conditions were under very good control."

Restacking the unburnt wood is one of the toughest jobs on the mountain," said Madsen. "It is hotter than hell and messy."

Certainly, it was one of the dirtiest jobs. How to get the soot off was always the challenge. "It is inside your ears," said Carolyn Madsen. "And this is really oily stuff."

"All the orifices are filled with soot," added Larry Madsen. "You're spitting this stuff out of your mouth for a day and a half."

"Burning is miserable work," said Prestwood. "It is harder than using a chain saw. The heat is so bad. Through the years, I don't know how many cuffs I burned off my gloves.

Not only is restacking dirty, tough work, it is also dangerous work. When taking a rest, it is unwise to sit downhill of the burn piles. Sometimes a big log, called a roller, can break loose and come crashing down the slope.

Markeita knows the lesson well, because at one burn-and-stacking party, she said, "We were sitting there, taking a break and having a beer, when someone shouted 'roller.' We looked up the mountain to see this huge sucker coming down. Six of us went one way and Jim [Markeita's husband] went the other way. The roller smashed into his thigh."

Hedstrom said, "If it had hit me in the upper body, it probably would have killed me. But, it hit me right in the soft part of the thigh."

"We had a case when a big stump rolled out of a pile and rolled down the mountain right into a Volkswagen," said Madsen. "There wasn't anything we could do about it. We were all waving and yelling, then crunch."

"I claim the Lord looked over us on the mountain, because we've had a lot of real close calls," said Hedstrom.

In September 1970, the ski club signed a contract with Hansen Lumber Company (HLC) to remove the big fir logs.

Piles of wood stacked through the summer and fall are burned in the fall or winter.

Terms of the agreement stated that HLC would remove marketable trees from the area plus other trees as indicated by the ski club. HLC would construct roads to allow access of the hauling trucks. Also, they would pay the ski club $2 per 1,000 board feet as scaled by Hansen for payment of their cutters. A minimum payment of $1,000 was guaranteed, with $200 of that paid. All roads would be open for travel on weekend periods. HLC would use reasonable care in skidding the loading logs so that minimum disturbance of the ground surface took place. The tractors would work within the boundaries of the slopes being cleared. The ski club would be responsible for the removal of slash and unmarketable timber.

Strong said, "We kept this agreement for about 25 years…it saved us considerable effort."

Rocks and Stumps

In the early 1970s, the ski club embarked upon a major effort to clear the slopes of rocks and stumps.

Although J.O. Johnson had blasted many rocks on the slopes in the past, rocks still caused problems on many of the slopes. Milt Gillespie said, "We were losing a lot of good skiing because the slopes were so rough. Before we could ski, there had to be enough snow to cover them."

When Gillespie took a fall on Little Abner because of rocks and more rocks, and as he lay on the slope for nearly half an hour feeling nauseated, he "swore vengeance on rocks."

Gillespie, Bob Rohwer, and Bob's wife, Audrey, declared Tuesday night as "blasting night." Gillespie said,"We did that all summer for a good many years."

"Gordon went to a garden supply house and bought a 100-lb. sack of ammonium nitrate. We bought some diesel oil and mixed it all up. We stuffed it back up underneath a big old stump with a stick of dynamite to start it," said Johnson. "With 100 lbs. of explosives, we worried about traffic, so we stopped the cars a long way up the road. When we pushed the button, the dynamite went off, but the ammonium nitrate fertilizer didn't. All it did was scatter a lot of fertilizer around. The grass still grows real good in that spot."

Though blasting is dangerous, for the most part the Rohwers, Gillespie, and Johnson experienced few scary incidents. But not all blasts went according to the blasters' prediction.

Johnson was introduced to blasting when Gordon Smith was president of the ski club. Gradually, he took over "blowing rocks." He recalled the story about a very troublesome boulder, twice as big as a large dining room table, on the Beginner's Slope.

"One day, the jackhammer crew drilled a couple of holes at an angle in that boulder. Dean Taylor and I shoved about three sticks of dynamite down each hole. We ran some prima cord so the sticks of dynamite would explode simultaneously. I didn't use a fuse. I used electric caps. I had about 50 feet of line. We got into a bunch of trees and I hit the wires. The whole damn rock, all the pieces, went straight up in the air. Seemed like 5,000 feet. Then, after an appreciable period of time, these huge boulders started to come down all around us. We could hear them crashing. Dean pushed me into this big tree."

Johnson remembered that the ammonium nitrate fertilizer explosives were just being invented. But since dynamite was expensive, Smith thought the new explosives were worth trying.

"Gordon went to a garden supply house and bought a 100-lb. sack of ammonium nitrate. We bought some diesel oil and mixed it all up. We stuffed it back up underneath a big old stump with a stick of dynamite to start it," said Johnson. "With 100 lbs. of explosives, we worried about traffic, so we stopped the cars a long way up the road. When we pushed the button, the dynamite went off, but the ammonium nitrate fertilizer didn't. All it did was scatter a lot of fertilizer around. The grass still grows real good in that spot."

"Currently, an explosive Kine-pak is used," said Strong.

Gillespie said, "It is a two-component explosive: ammonium nitrate, which is like flour, and nitro methane. Until the components are mixed together, they are not explosive. It is safer than dynamite. It is a fairly potent explosive that is far less sensitive than dynamite and considerably more powerful."

Kathy Gillespie, Milt's wife, had 200 lbs. of the unmixed Kine-pak in the trunk of her Volvo when her car was rear ended by a big pickup truck in Santa Fe. When a policeman arrived to investigate the collision, she said, "'Mum' was the word."

Bob Rohwer felt comfortable working with explosives. "I'm quite happy with the explosives. Sometimes I'm kind of a harum-scarum guy, but when I work with powder I do it by the numbers," said Rohwer.

But Rohwer's old green Bronco took some rocks after a blast on the slope called Breathless. Though the Bronco was parked at some distance away, Rohwer said, "the rocks arched up over the trees. The tailgate on the Bronco took a hit, smashing the glass. Another skull-sized rock put a dent in the roof." His insurance paid for the damage. Rohwer was amazed that the insurance company never questioned how a rock smashed his tailgate and ripped the metal in the roof.

Blasting broke up the boulders but still left rocks on the slopes. "Getting rid of those rocks was more than three people could handle," said Gillespie. "We began to organize rock-rolling crews."

Gillespie said the most memorable rock-rolling crew was headed by Sig Hecker, who later became the Laboratory's director. He'd have 20 or 30 people to help. Sometimes it would take two people with a pry bar to force the rock from the ground. "It was impressive to watch," said Gillespie.

Sig Hecker working on the mountain. He headed the most memorable rock-rolling crew.

"That was the most fun on Bonanza to watch those humongous rocks go down and cut a swath through the trees a foot and a half in diameter. It was like there was nothing there at all," said Stan Moore.

"That giant pile of rocks at the bottom of Bonanza where it turns into the traverse—that's half the rocks his crew rolled off Bonanza," said Gillespie.

Then there was the case of the mysterious rock, not a result of blasting. Gillespie said a crew was working on the second road on one of the slopes. Someone (we blamed each other) kicked a rock loose. It started rolling toward an International Scout that was driving slowly across the slopes. The scene unfolded in slow motion. "There was time for some discussion about where the rock would hit the Scout," said Gillespie.

A disk-shaped rock cut through the first layer of steel and embedded itself in the middle of the driver's door. "Had it been a few inches higher, it would have gone through the window and gotten somebody's head," said Gillespie. "The driver was pretty philosophical about the incident," said Gillespie. "He drove up to where we were standing, got out, looked at the rock, and looked at us. We all kind of said, 'Mmmmmmm, looks like a rock.'"

Blasting works for boulders but not for stumps. The stump may shatter when blasted, but usually the shards of the stump remain attached to their roots. Thus a crew using chain saws has to cut the shards and roots.

The ski club finally invested in a $2,000 stump chipper. "It was one heck of a machine," said Gillespie.

"A combination of blasting, rock rolling, and chipping stumps enabled us to open the area earlier with less snow," said Gillespie.

What's in a Name?

Spreading straw on the slopes covers small rocks and encourages the growth of grass. This provides a better skiing surface when snow cover is thin.

Why Lone Spruce, Wildcat, Porcupine, Pussycat, Big Mother, Sidewinder, Why Not, I Don't Care, or One More Time? Who named the slopes and what are the stories behind the names? Can all the stories be told?

The first three major slopes to be cut were Lumberyard, Aspen, and the Racing Slope, now called Mal's Run.

Lumberyard likely acquired its moniker because the ski club lacked time to stack all the timber. Stretch Fretwell said the trees were felled down the fall line of the slope, as neatly as possible, and trimmed of their branches. Originally, the ski club planned to leave the logs in place, but aspen shoots grew between the crevices, causing dangerous ski conditions. Also, the Forest Service thought the logs posed unsafe ski conditions. The logs were removed but the name, Lumberyard, stuck.

The name for Aspen Slope was a natural. In the late 1800s, a great fire swept through Pajarito Mountain, destroying many of the conifers, spruce, and fir trees. Aspen trees, with a sprawling, interrelated root system, quickly grew into the burnt areas. On the slope west of Lumberyard stood great stands of the quaking poplars. It seemed logical to name the slope after the trees with quivering leaves of gold. To this day, volunteers continue the war against aspen shoots.

Though Fretwell wasn't part of the pioneer cutting crew, he said he had the privilege of naming Spring Pitch. "It was slightly concave. I thought there might be a spring under the big rocks at the bottom. Also, it reminded me a little bit of Spring Pitch at Aspen, Colorado," he said. But Fretwell said the slopes were usually named by the cutters.

Thorn said, "We had a democracy. Everyone who helped cut the trees down got to name the slopes." However, when Thorn was cutting Wildcat, some people thought the slope should be called "Bobcat." Thorn resisted the suggestion. "I didn't want to call it Bobcat because that's my name. I said, 'Let's call it Wildcat,' so that's what we did," he said.

Prestwood said, "Pussycat got its name because, I think, it was so easy compared to Wildcat."

After Wildcat was cut, the cutting crew turned their efforts to the east of the Beginner's Slope. That was when the ski club began to think about expanding in that direction and installing a lift.

"We did a lot of cutting in 1964," said Thorn. That's when the lumberjacks cut Daisy Mae, named after the female star of the popular comic strip, Li'l Abner.

Thorn said, "Of course, again the wood was green. We burned on Thanksgiving, in the snow, while everyone else was skiing."

Rene Prestwood recalled the event. "There were 42 piles of wood on the Daisy Mae traverse and further down the slope. I don't think pile 42 ever got burned. The snow got so deep by the time we got down there, we couldn't find the pile. People were making turns off it. It took us six days to burn 41 piles of wood. That Thanksgiving weekend, we spent it hauling 5-gallon cans of kerosene, between our legs, up the T-bar, then skidding them behind us to fill the burners. While everyone else was skiing, we were burning. We were a little bit ticked."

The following year, the cutters started on Li'l Abner. Eventually, they would cut Dog Patch, the fictional hollow in the comic strip where Li'l Abner and Daisy Mae lived.

Thorn said, "By the time we had widened Daisy Mae and Li'l Abner to the point where we could have enough slope to provide some skiing of the area, we did put in a chair lift."

When Lone Spruce fell to the chain saws, the cutters left a beautiful, large single spruce tree on the slope. Prestwood said, "We left it on purpose so we could call it Lone Spruce."

Strong said, "Bob Thorn took special care to protect that lone spruce, but when the chair lift was installed on the slope in 1969, Bob asked Tony Sowder of Riblet (the safety person who checked on the lifts) what he thought of the tree. Tony's response was that if it was his lift, he would cut the tree down. The tree came down and was replaced by the sign post."

Usually a slope was named while the lumberjacks took a break for a beer. Such was the day when Thorn and his cutting crew sat at the top of the mountain with beers in their hands. As they looked down the slope between Dog Patch and Bonanza, Madsen remembered Thorn saying, "I've always wanted to name a slope Sundance."

At the top of Sundance is a patch of ski area the cutters will always call "Oh Shit Park," though it doesn't appear on the ski area map.

A fellow by the name of Adams was hired by Hansen to cut Sundance and Dog Patch. Ron Strong said, "Adams was about seventy. He had a CP 125 McCulloch saw. It was the same kind of saw that Bob carried around when he was in his prime."

When Adams set out to cut the trees on Sundance, there was some confusion about the markings. The trees had been marked with ribbons, yellow and blue.

Thorn said, "We told Adams to follow the yellow on the right and the blue on the left. He went the wrong way. We thought he'd go from the bottom up, but he went from the top down."

Harry Flaugh said, "Adams worked for two days. When we went up to see how it was going, he had cut down the trees we wanted left. Ron walked over there and said, 'Oh, shit!'"

Prestwood said, "There is a huge wide area before you get to Bonanza. Well, that is not supposed to be there. There were supposed to be cuts in the trees, like when you ski over to Boomer

Skiesta

Skiesta is an end-of-ski-season spring festival, usually held in mid to late March when the weather tends to be warm. Costumes are encouraged, and young and old turn out for the tee-pee race and the Sloppy Slalom, both held on the Beginner's Slope. Other events, such as a jumping contest and mogul-mashing contest, a giant slalom and a downhill race, tend to attract the more advanced skiers. Lift operators often enter the shovel race, where they straddle their shovels and ride them, at hair-raising speeds, down Lone Spruce. The ski club provides food, beverages, and live music, and if the weather cooperates, a good time is had by all.

(1)

(2)

(3)

(4)

(5)

(6)

Skiesta Over the Years

1. Bob Thorn, dressed as a Girl Scout, enjoys Skiesta with his daughter, Andrea, and her friend, Tracy Flaugh, dressed as boxes of cookies; 2. a large crowd enjoys a sunny Skiesta; 3. Brian Riepe, a penguin, races down the mountain; 4. Mike Riepe, also a penguin, snowplows through a "tee-pee" gate; 5. eager contestents wait for John Rogers to announce the winner of a contest; 6. a costumed crowd watches a competitor in an event.

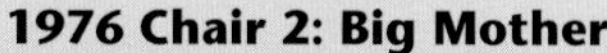

A Chair Chronology

1969 Chair 1: Lone Spruce

The lift selection committee, Dean Taylor and Bob Thorn, chose a Riblet Tramway Company double chair with a capacity to service 1200 skiers per hour and chose Gerald Martin as the installation contractor. In June 1969, installation of the lift began and was completed by December 1969 at a total cost of $125,000.

Volunteers even climb to the top of the towers to tighten bolts.

The contractor encountered difficulty when he tried various methods of digging holes, including drilling, for the towers. He settled on hand digging as the best method for the task.

Ron Strong said, "The ski club president, Phil Reinig, had a case of champagne set aside for the completion of the chair. It was after dark when the load test was finished. There were only a few club members left and more than enough champagne to go around."

Those remaining ski club members enjoyed the first ride on Chair No. 1 that night, under the stars, sipping their champagne.

Rene Prestwood said the ramp on the Spruce chair was designed by Thorn. "We joked, wondering if it was strong enough," he said. "It only had 31 telephone poles in it. We told him you could land a 747 on the thing."

1976 Chair 2: Big Mother

A second chair lift was installed in 1976. Dean Taylor, Ron Strong, Jack Travis, and Carl Young served on the lift selection committee. Again, a Riblet Tramway Company double chair was selected, and again Gerald Martin was the installation contractor. An acquaintance of Ron Strong's, Jim Sullivan, considered a knowledgeable person, was hired by Gerald Martin as the supervisor for the chair installation. (Later, Sullivan would install a Riblets at Angel Fire.)

Skiers enjoy a ride up the Big Mother chair.

According to Strong, the installation proceeded in orderly fashion. Of course, digging the holes was always a challenge. Strong said, "Some were dug with a backhoe. Tower no. 9 required blasting. The remaining holes were dug by hand." When it came time to install the towers, on-the-job ingenuity ruled the moment.

Strong recalled, "Jim had been trying to locate a helicopter for tower installation. After the tower bases were in, we were notified that a chopper would be passing through New Mexico on its way from South America and could be used if we were ready. The chopper arrived and started flying. Unfortunately, the towers were in the lower parking lot with bottomless dust. The dust clogged the helicopter's inlet filters. While the filters were being cleaned, the towers were moved to the

Beginner's Slope using the John Deere bulldozer. The flying then proceeded. It turned out that this was the first lift that the pilot had flown and also the first for the construction crew except for Jim. Because of confusing communications, the pilot released the sling on tower no. 11 before the nuts were threaded sufficiently on the bolts. The tower fell, bending the flanges and damaging the sheave train attachment on one side. Flying was held up until the communication problems were worked out. The remaining towers were then set. A couple of towers that could be set with a boom truck from roads were set later. Also on tower no. 11, flanges were straightened and the machinery replaced. The tower was reset using the boom truck since, fortunately, it was near a road."

The installation of chair lifts requires the ski patrol to learn how to evacuate them.

The load test on the chair was performed on the same day as the fall work party and the barbecue. "After the barbecue, work party attendees were invited to take an inaugural ride," said Strong. Piles of slash on Big Mother were still burning as the riders rode the chair to the top of Pajarito Mountain and returned at dusk. The embers glowed beneath them as the view of the Rio Grande Valley spread before them.

1981 and 1982 Chairs 3 and 4

Ron Strong wrote that the installation of the next two lifts was driven by the perception of many members of the ski club that lift lines were excessive and there was a need for additional lift capacity. As a result, a previous vote, authorizing new lodge construction, was reversed. The ski club membership voted to replace the T-bar and to install a beginners lift by 1981.

Chair no. 3, which services the Beginner's Slope, is a double chair with a 1,200 skier capacity per hour. The installation cost was $229,000.

Chair no. 4, the Aspen chair, replaced the 20-year-old T-bar in 1982. The triple chair has the capacity to carry 1550 skiers per hour. The tower bases were mostly dug by hand. The concrete for most of the towers was flown to the bases by helicopter. The installation cost was $511,000.

1994 Chair 5: Townsight

The Townsight chair lift was installed in 1994. All the tower holes were dug with a tracked excavator. Tower no. 9 required some blasting. Concrete was flown to six towers, one-quarter yard at a time, by a small Hughes chopper. The chopper was towed down from Portland, Oregon, behind a truck. This cost roughly $1.25 per mile.

On the day the towers were installed, it rained and snowed but cleared off long enough to complete the job, which took two hours.

The quadruple chair has the capacity to carry 1,650 skiers per hour. The installation cost was about $800,000.

The lift selection committee was Bill Cox, Ed Hoth, John Tegtmeier, Dean Taylor, and Ron Strong.

The base of the Townsight lift is installed.

and Townsight. The whole area got cut down. Well, it was just a misunderstanding."

But because of this mistake, the cutters worried that the wind would scour that huge open area and would cause the slopes to be unskiable. Thorn said, "From the beginning, we thought a great deal about the wind. On Compromise, the wind just tore up through a little gully and wiped out the snow, and before Wildcat was widened, the wind funneled down through a narrow opening and just scoured the snow off the top."

Prestwood said, "Our original concept of what would happen really didn't. We've never had a problem with snow on top of Sundance and Dog Patch."

Myrna Strong cuts aspen shoots and tall grass with a "gillyswisher," a weed-eater type of a device with a saw blade strong enough to cut through cane-like bushes. Margaret Flaugh works in the background.

Thorn said, "There were going to be two slopes around Sundance, but after the mistake, we improvised. In a picture, you can see some offsets right at the top. Finally, we got Adams straightened out and headed in the right direction."

Strong said, "Adams was a vigorous old guy. He also cut Pussycat and a lot of Big Mother."

It was Hansen's caterpillar operator who inspired the name, Big Mother.

"Elmer was a character," said Prestwood. "He didn't have any teeth, and he chewed tobacco. The only time he wore his teeth was when he took his wife out for dinner. He was an old 'cat skinner' from way back. He was one of those guys where every other word was the F-word. Well, when we cut trees on Big Mother, they were huge."

Ron Strong said that when the cutters started to clear the slope to get it ready for a lift, it kept getting wider and wider and bigger and bigger.

Prestwood said, "Elmer was up there dragging those big trees with the cat. Every other word was mother f—r. That's all he talked about all day. So, Thorn jokingly said, 'Why don't we call this slope Mother F—r.' Of course, that was on the raw side, so we thought, to compromise, we'd call the slope Big Mother."

Once they had cut Big Mother, Prestwood said, "We cut Nuther Mother between Sidewinder, which moved around like a snake, and Big Mother. And, if you don't want to go down Oops, a short, steep slope, then there is Easy Mother, which the ladies didn't think was an appropriate name for a slope, but it stuck."

Nan Moore, Gene's wife, said, "No! We didn't like the mother names. We fussed and fussed about every one of them, but it didn't stop them."

When the cutters decided to mark out an area between Porcupine Park and Wildcat, and reconfigure Porcupine Park, they met opposition from ski club members.

Strong said that, at that time, Porcupine Park went all the way down to Two Fingers.

Prestwood said, "There was an argument whether to cut the trees in Porcupine Park." Strong said that the issue came to a vote by the ski club. "It was kind of a fifty-fifty decision, so we decided to change our plan and leave Porcupine Park."

"Compromise was a compromise because some people wanted to ski trees and others weren't so hot on the trees. So the alternative was to cut Compromise and Bob's Bowl." said Prestwood.

As for Three Fingers, which used to be Two Fingers, Prestwood said, "We couldn't ski Two Fingers until the snow was quite deep to cover the huge rocks, so Harry Flaugh decided to cut a little valley right alongside of Two Fingers. He called that valley Harry's Finger." But Three Fingers held forth. Harry's slope is Why Harry.

Prestwood said that the telephone line goes through Ma Bell, thus the name.

Gene Moore remembered a funny story about his slope, Gene's Choice, which he says wasn't his choice, even though Thorn said it was.

"Well, I had been helping cut for several years. Ron, Harry, and Bob always laid out the slopes. One day Bob said, 'Well, Gene, your time to lay this one out.' It was up above Camp May, so I walked it out and used the paint to mark it off. I think they redid it almost completely. It was spring, and all four of us were walking around. I'd say 'well, I think it should go this way,' or Let's move it a little bit.' They made the decision to go one way or another. Bob told me that was my slope, so for a good while, we tried to think of a name with Gene in it."

Bruce Gavett, left, and Rene Prestwood enjoy a joke during a break. Bruce was the first area manager hired at Pajarito Mountain, and Rene can be given credit for naming several of the slopes after his risqué jokes.

Finally, Thorn named the slope Gene's Choice.

Breathless and Precious?

Prestwood said that one afternoon, about three o'clock, when the gang was working, they'd get "kind of silly and start telling jokes." Prestwood said Breathless and Precious came from a risqué joke that he told, but the joke isn't printable.

Likewise, Why Not, One More Time, and I Don't Care got kicked around one afternoon while the cutters were sitting around the lodge drinking beer and telling off-color jokes.

Salamander Gully, not an actual slope but a trail back to the lifts or lodge, acquired its name because of the Jemez Salamander, an endangered species. Ten had been found on the eastern and lower elevations of the 106-acre tract of ski area land.

To protect the Jemez Salamander, the Forest Service recommended that the slopes not be cut in one direction but there should be sections of forest left to stand where they live. Thus, the Confusions (East Confusion, Mid Confusion, and West Confusion) were cut to make a crisscross of interconnected islands. Also, Flaugh said the membership wanted some slopes with more character.

Larry Madsen said that Mushroom originally had a narrow opening at the top, but the slope widened in the middle, where Elmer Hansen had taken out the big trees. For a while, there weren't any signs at the top, so most people didn't know the slope was there between Lone Spruce and Racing Slope.

Likewise, Why Not, One More Time, and I Don't Care got kicked around one afternoon while the cutters were sitting around the lodge drinking beer and telling off-color jokes.

"It was hidden away in the dark," said Madsen, "so the name Mushroom."

Flaugh said, "On powder days, we skied Mushroom, and then skied the old rope tow trail that went up through there."

"Townsight got its name because it looks over the town," said Prestwood.

Unlike Nevershine Hill, a portion of Camp May Road that never sees the sun, Evershine Ridge, on the east side of Pajarito Mountain, gets lots of sun.

Rim Run speaks for itself.

Bruce's Boulevard was named for the Pajarito ski area's first full-time general manager, Bruce Gavett.

Ron's Run, named by the lumberjacks for Ron Strong, is part of lower Sundance.

The slope called Hedache, on the east side of the mountain, honors lumberjack Jim Hedstrom and his wife, Markeita, head burner.

Hindsight was an afterthought.

Boomer has two stories.

Kathy Gillespie, Margaret Flaugh, and other wives believed a slope needed to have a name kids could associate with, thus Boomer, but Markeita Hedstrom doesn't believe the women had any say in the naming of the slopes.

But Larry Madsen remembered the story this way. One day, while the lumberjacks were cutting Boomer, they sat down to have a beer. Someone asked the question, "What should we name the slope?"

They looked out to the Sangres in the distance and the town and the Laboratory below. Certainly, bomb business was associated with the Laboratory. People started tossing out names.

"How about TNT?"

"La Bomba sounds good to me."

"Boom, Boom is good," said another.

After a few more beers and a play on bomb words, the group settled on Boomer.

In the late seventies, Lone Spruce lift serves several runs on the east side, while the Big Mother lift provides the opportunity to expand toward the West. The Valle Grande is visible behind the mountain.

By 1988 the only part of the mountain not yet developed is the "far east" (the left side of the photograph).

In fact, Flaugh said that when they started naming the slopes, the group thought it would be interesting to name some of them after test shots conducted at the Nevada Test Site. But he said only about two percent of the skiers would know what the names meant.

If they had followed up on that idea, skiers would have become familiar with names such as Mighty Oak, Tulia, Mini Jade, Toril, Whiteface, Floydada, Bowie, Gnome, Gasbuggy, Ranger, and Trinity, to name just a few possibilities.

The Ski Patrol*

The Los Alamos Ski Patrol has been inseparable from the ski club from the beginning during the 1947–48 ski season, when its founders realized the increasing need for a dedicated group to assist injured or lost skiers, promote safety on the mountain, and insure a continuing pool of trained volunteers. Many of the hard-working volunteers responsible for the club growth were also to be found on the patrol roster.

The patrol promptly affiliated with the National Ski Patrol System (NSPS), which at the time was only 10 years older than the Los Alamos patrol, in part to benefit from their accumulated training materials and standards. Since then the patrol has evolved and expanded to keep pace with club developments and an ever-changing ski industry. The trend toward a commercial-like operation on Pajarito Mountain carried with it increased requirements for patrol skills and organization, expressed in more rigorous training and testing and the inevitable paperwork. Various operational plans and procedures were developed over the years to deal with foreseeable activities on the mountain. Patrol bylaws were first drafted and approved in 1982 and update in 1996 to account for the continuous evolution. Patrollers are also human though: a newsletter of the 1981–82 season reminded them of the ban on skiing between the T-bar and the tree line to the west and noted that enforcement would be difficult unless patrollers set a good example for the membership.

In the small photo, the base facilites for the ski patrol are shown as they existed before volunteers built an addition.

After the move to Pajarito Mountain and the eventual construction of the building now known as the "old" lodge, the patrol occupied space in the lower level of the lodge, facing the parking lot. Before long, the need for a separate building for the patrol became clear. That site, downhill from the old lodge, is still the patrol room,

**The section about the ski patrol was written by Bill Chambers, long-time ski patroller and ski club member.*

although considerably expanded by major additions in the summers of 1993 and 1994. A toilet and plumbing with hot water was hailed as a major breakthrough. Earlier, as the Aspen chair began operation in the 1982–83 season, a warming hut for patrollers and equipment was deemed necessary at the top of the Aspen lift to improve accident response times across ever-expanding skiable terrain. The club approved $3,000 for material, and the Aspen Haus blossomed in the summer of 1984. At first the heat came from propane, but eventually a commercial antenna system was built just up the hill and electricity came to the Aspen Haus. As with most of the mountain construction, dedicated volunteers from the patrol and club membership provided the muscle for all these events.

Patrollers keep their skills up to date by participating in training on the mountain.

Training and testing for returning patrollers and new candidates stretched instructor resources to the limit. Fall and winter training sessions were conducted in skills including winter emergency care, CPR, chair lift evacuation, and toboggan handling skills. In the eighties, patrol rosters exceeded 100, with new candidate classes reaching 15 to 20 adults and juniors. The junior patrol reached into the local high school with substantial appeal and produced young patrollers with many talents. Besides taking full part in mountain operations, after completing their basic training, the juniors raised funds to help send teams to the annual regional and national junior patrol seminars and consistently took top awards in the skill competitions. They never seemed daunted by the extra weight toted by patrollers on duty, averaging 36 pounds of gear in one set of random measurements.

Meanwhile, the operations during the winter season grew in size and complexity. Average accident rates were roughly three per operating day, with larger and larger fractions being non-resident daily ticket holders. Of course, the rate fluctuated greatly—from a number of zeros on Wednesday to a probably record-setting weekend in the 1992–93 season, with 14 accidents on Saturday and 12 on Sunday. Approximately two out of three of the accidents required evacuations from the mountain to the patrol room by toboggan. Tragically, the patrollers have had to

Work Party

The annual work party and barbecue is held in the fall, after a busy summer on the mountain and before the first snow falls. This is a good opportunity for typical club members—who may not have the time, interest, or skill to volunteer on the mountain on a regular basis—to join in for a few hours of hard work. Usually, they are expected to roll rocks or stack cut wood and slash into piles for burning. Adults and children frequently turn out to put in a day's work. In the late afternoon, the ski club provides a hearty meal. For years, J.O. Johnson spent an entire day and night pit roasting the pork, and the wives of many of the regular volunteers and ski club board members often contributed the salads, beans, and other fixings. A hearty meal was the reward for a day spent working on the hill among trees in their fall splendor.

While some volunteers work on the mountain, others "supervise" the roasting of meat in a pit barbecue, until everyone eats at the end of the day.

deal with the occasional fatality, including two ex-patrollers who suffered fatal heart attacks while skiing at the area.

During the 1985–86 season, the patrol got its first snowmobile, which proved to be a great asset for mountain logistics as well as in assisting toboggan evacuations from the low spots. Naturally, snowmobile operations added yet another step to the education of a basic patroller, particularly in view of the prompt demise of that first machine in an encounter with a tree.

The "New" Lodge

"Don't hold it; vote for a new ski lodge."

In a letter to the *Los Alamos Monitor* in 1987, Judy Young, a ski patroller, wrote:

"Why is a new lodge currently proposed for a vote? I don't think of it as a Colorado type ski lodge; I dream of a secure storage area, a rental shop that doesn't drip on your head, not an office for the mountain manager that only a mole could love and a gopher could find, and wow! A 20th Century toilet, and a place to wash my hands before I clean off your ski-edge wound. I have to use the facilities several times during the day. I'm not very good at 'holding it' until I get home. Think about it please, before the vote deadline May 7, 1987."

A majority of the membership agreed with Judy. The new lodge was approved in a mail ballot by a vote of 503 to 123.

The approval was significant because twice a proposal for a new lodge had been presented to the membership for a vote and twice it had been defeated. First, when the west land became available for purchase. Again, when "a vocal majority of the club's members felt improvements to existing ski trails and creation of new trails was a higher priority."

"We were at the point with the outside toilets that we were getting a reputation of being interested in the core skiers who accepted that style of life, and that affected members as well as outside skiers," said Gary Wall. "It was time to move into the new century—for the women especially."

At a meeting on July 30, 1987, the Board of Directors selected Architecture Plus, Inc. of Los Alamos to design the lodge and to build the shell. Wall said that the lodge committee had interviewed prospective architects, but chose Roger Camillo, a local architect who had ties with the ski club. The committee liked his unique design for the lodge.

"It was a break from the construction tradition we had on the ski hill—keep it simple," said Wall. "The proposal was a new type of construction, using pre-fabricated panels. It was an interesting architectural proposal instead of just a shed, a box with a tin roof."

Wall said that the architectural firm was to act as the general contractor to do the initial construction, the foundation, and the shell. Ski club members would finish the interior, which would house a ski rental shop, ticket window, a cafeteria, dining area, restrooms, a deck on the main floor, a balcony dining area on the third floor, office space, a caretaker's apartment, and ski equipment lockers to be rented by ski club members. At the time, Wall thought it would take two years to complete the 13,000-square-foot lodge.

The shell of the new lodge is built in 1987; the completed lodge before the deck is installed.

A loan for the construction of the shell was secured from Los Alamos National Bank. To finance the rest of the project, the ski club planned to use monies from yearly income.

Construction of the lodge began on August 13, 1987. Within nine months, the shell phase of the new lodge was nearly completed. Gary Wall agreed to oversee all aspects of the interior finishing. "John Hopson, then president of the ski club, twisted my arm," said Wall. "With the shell finalized, we started in earnest with the volunteer work."

Crew chiefs were selected to organize volunteers to work on the deck, the interior framing, plumbing, electricity, sheetrock installation, ceiling installation, and painting. Meanwhile, volunteers had been busy working on the water system for the mountain. "There was the water tank and putting in the septic system," said Wall. "Just digging that project was challenging in itself—lots of rocks."

"We spent most of the summer up there, and because the ski season was late, we continued to work heavy duty through February," said Wall. "We worked weekends and at least one evening during the week."

Larry Madsen remembered a conversation with Bob Thorn concerning the lodge. Thorn said that somebody had to do the job, so several of the volunteers agreed to quit one year of cutting to build the lodge. "I don't think anyone realized what a damned job it was. But we weren't about to give up. We were going to finish it," said Madsen.

"It was pretty tough," said Harry Flaugh.

"The guys were gone all the time," said Markeita Hedstrom.

June Wall, then newly married to Gary, said, "Those years, building the lodge, seemed like ten years of volunteering."

Nevertheless, June often provided barbecues for the lodge workers. She brought up hamburgers and cooked them for the crew. She even laid treads on the stairs.

"It was a family affair in a lot of respects. We were a core group up there doing whatever needed to be done," said Wall. "But over that long haul, where people spend that kind of time together, there was some pressure and flare-ups—feuds and things that had to be settled between people."

Top: Paul Guthals and Milt Gillespie build stairs from the parking lot to the lodge. Bottom: A new deck connects the new lodge with the old lodge and provides lots of space for skiers to relax and enjoy a sunny day.

Even though completing the lodge required a much greater effort than the volunteers had bargained for, success was theirs as was reported in the *LASC Newsletter* of February 27, 1989:

"Thanks to the yeomanly efforts of Gary Wall and the many other volunteer workers, the deck, bathrooms and rental shop in the new lodge were ready to use on opening day. With additional hard work, we were given an occupancy permit for the rest of the lodge (excepting the cafeteria) in time to open the dining area for the February 4–5 weekend. The lodge is a superb example of the tremendous contributions of the active club volunteers, and a facility we can all be proud of for many years to come."

The newsletter also thanked Pete Pyburn of Ironmaster and Dave Smith of LA Enterprises. "These two companies purchased most of the materials for the plumbing and electrical work and performed many of the most demanding tasks for a reasonable fee. The club is grateful for their valuable help."

"Building the lodge turned out to be more of a commitment than I had bargained for, but on the other hand, there were a lot of key crew chief people who helped make the whole thing work," said Wall. "Following the project, we organized a windjammer cruise. We invited friends and lodge workers. About one-third of the passengers on the trip were from Los Alamos. It was our celebration."

"Old Blue"

Bob Thorn's 1969 Dodge, Old Blue, "used and abused," was the designated "ski hill truck." A six-passenger, crew-cab truck with four-wheel drive, it hauled workers, chain saws, gas cans, and coolers filled with beer up and down the mountain.

Thorn's blue truck served the ski club well for over 30 years.

Thorn's daughter, Kyle Wheeler, remembered one incident in Old Blue that was pretty freightening. One evening she and her father drove to Pajarito Mountain to check on burn piles near the top of Compromise. The ground was snow covered and slick. Even though Old Blue had four-wheel drive, conditions required chains on all four tires. While they tended the burn piles near the top of the mountain, snow continued to fall.

When they drove down the mountain, in pitch-black darkness, Kyle said, "I could feel the truck slipping. I was most frightened when we were crossing the slopes, because if we slipped off the road, we could tumble a long way before stopping. My heart was in my throat most of the way down."

When they reached the bottom of the mountain, Thorn discovered that one of rear chains had broken loose. Kyle was glad she didn't know that before they reached the safety of a regular road.

Although Old Blue was Thorn's personal truck, he often loaned it to the lumberjacks when he was traveling on Laboratory business.

Harry Flaugh remembered one time when Thorn was on travel, he and Ron Strong were on the mountain in Old Blue, near the old gas house that used to be near where the ski school buildings now stand. Flaugh said, "We were on a hill. Ron was driving. We stopped. He put it in gear. We got out, and we were only a few steps away when the truck started rolling toward the road. Ron tried to jump into the truck to put on the brakes, but he couldn't make it. Old Blue smashed into a large aspen tree, jamming the radiator back into the fan."

Flaugh said that he and Ron just stood there looking at each other. Since the radiator had leaked fluid, they wondered: How would we get Old Blue back home? And what were we going to tell Bob?

In his own vehicle, Flaugh followed Ron, who was driving Old Blue. "Ron would run the motor a little bit. Then he would stop the engine and coast, so it wouldn't get hot," said Flaugh.

At 10 p.m., they finally coasted into Metzger's gas station where they filled the radiator with water. Then they drove Old Blue to Strong's house where they checked it over for further damage. The hood's latch had been damaged and the doors sprung. Flaugh said that while they were trying to pry open the hood, a taxi drove past them. "Suddenly the taxi stops and backs up right beside us," he said. Inside the taxi is Thorn, returning from business travel to Europe.

Strong said, "Bob rolls down the window. He asks, 'What's going on?' His eyes get wide. He says, 'I shouldn't have asked.' He rolls up the window and drives off."

Another story surrounding the truck is about Coors and Budweiser beer.

One day late in November, the cutters were on the mountain, finishing some stacking and burning, throwing charred branches into the trees, trying to get the slopes ready for winter. Larry Madsen and Thorn were in Old Blue, driving along an upper road when a terrible knocking sound came from the truck. Madsen recalled that Bob had been on travel for a few weeks and when he got out of the truck to check the oil, Bob said, "I can't trust this truck to anybody."

Madsen said, "We scrounged around in the back of the truck, poured in two quarts of chain-saw oil, managed to turn Old Blue around, got to the bottom of the mountain, and filled it full of oil."

But on that day, adventures with Old Blue weren't over. Thorn and Madsen drove back up the mountain to where the crews were working. Madsen said, "We're up there where the road crosses Racing Slope. Now, smoke comes out from under the hood. Thorn said, 'What now?'"

The radiator was dry so it was overheating. Madsen said that he started throwing snow on the radiator to cool it down. They managed to fill a beer can with some water which they poured into the radiator. Madsen recalled Thorn saying, "at this rate, we're going to be here all day so let's have a beer."

Bob Thorn stands on the stump of a tree he felled. For many, many years, he was the "chief cutter" and led a team of dedicated and hardworking men who called themselves the "Rat Pack."

In the back of Old Blue was a case of Coors and a case of Budweiser. Madsen thought it was a good idea to drink the Budweiser and pour the Coors into the radiator. "We poured in seven cans of Coors. We joked that we ought to have a picture of this to send to Budweiser—pouring Coors into the radiator and drinking Budweiser. Thorn's only concern was that the beer would foam-up and come out of the radiator. It worked great,"Madsen said.

During the ski season, the first vehicle parked by the T-bar in the morning and the last to leave in the evening was Old Blue.

"About 30 minutes before the lift opened, there was Bob and Rene having a little hearty burgundy," said Madsen. "We had a real routine. Had wine before we got on the lift. We always broke about

10:30 a.m. We'd hear Rene say, 'Geez, Bob, I think this is a wine run.' Bob says, 'Yeah, I think this is a wine run.' So we'd ski on down and pile into Old Blue and break out the plastic glasses. If it was a nice day, we put them on the hood. Then we'd make a few runs before lunch, then back up on the mountain. We always broke in the middle of the afternoon."

"Yeah, we had another wine break," said Flaugh.

Madsen said, "We always talked about cutting a slope called 'Wine Run' but we could never figure out where to put it."

After many years, Thorn deeded Old Blue to Pajarito Mountain. The doors are latched with bungee cords. The floorboard has rust holes. But still it runs, having provided "30 years of hard service."

Strong said, "It's got a strong heart, just like Bob."

But Thorn's heart eventually failed, burdened by the cancer he was diagnosed with in 1984. He died in 1990.

Kyle Wheeler said, "When my dad died, his friends and family assembled on Pajarito Mountain to scatter his ashes. Old Blue was called upon to carry Dad on his final journey to a suitable resting place near the top of Pajarito. Fully loaded with people who loved Bob, Old Blue went up the mountain as it had thousands of times before, but this time a long line of vehicles followed behind, filled with people very sad to be saying goodbye to a pioneer of Pajarito Mountain. When Dad's ashes were spread on Bob's Bowl by his good friend Harry Flaugh, the rest of us toasted his memory with Budweiser."

Pajarito Mountain Spared by the Cerro Grande Fire

May 10, 2000

How did the largest widefire in the state of New Mexico, fanned by extreme winds and fueled by dense forest, burn through 47,650 acres of Forest Service land, decimate the homes of nearly 400 families, yet spare the ski hill?

Bruce Gavett, now retired but then the general manager of the ski area, recalled the intense days before he and his crew were ordered to evacuate. "We worked side by side with the Forest Service and the firefighters doing whatever we could to save the ski area," said Gavett. As a Marine veteran of World War II, a miner, a pioneer in downhill skiing, and a former firefighter, Gavett knew that he and the others were in a struggle to stave off disaster.

The success of their efforts relied on the support system of helicopters and water tankers called in by the Forest Service. According to Gavett, when the fire would jump the road, they'd call in the helicopter to drop water and put it out. When they were frantically backburning behind the Lone Spruce lift, hot spots erupted. Once again, out went the call to the helicopter. Those calls continued for hours into days. Finally, the order to evacuate came when the crew was engaged in an effort to bulldoze a fire break near the bottom of Evershine Ridge, the easternmost slope on the mountain.

Gavett suggested that the water tankers be parked by the Lone Spruce chair lift and the Townsite chair lift. All other vehicles—the dozers, trucks, and ATVs—were parked in the center of the parking lot with their keys left in the ignitions in case the vehicles needed to be moved.

"We left believing we'd never see Pajarito Mountain nor the ski hill the same," said Gavett.

What saved the ski hill?

Several conditions contributed to its survival. The wind shifts were a major factor. Also, the slopes, developed by those who cut, bucked, slashed, and burned the timber, proved worthy as fire breaks. "Especially one slope," said Gavett. "If we hadn't had Evershine Ridge, we'd have lost a lot more on Pajarito Mountain than 80 acres." Though he can't be sure, Gavett said, "I believe the heroic efforts of the firefighters who manned those tankers may have saved our ski hill."

Sources

The material for this book came from numerous sources listed below. Many of these are available in the archives of the Los Alamos Historical Society and the Los Alamos Ski Club:

Interviews videotaped by Paul Allison, Jim "Stretch" Fretwell, and Dale Holm

Video #1 Darrah Nagle, Tom Putnam, John Orndoff, Bob Rohwer, Bill Jarmie, and Dale Holm

Video #2 Bill Jarmie, Dale Holm, Stirling Colgate, Wes Nichols, and Luther Richerson

Video #3 Rene Prestwood and Bob Thorn

Video #4 Henry Laquer, Perc King, and Bob Walker

Video #5 Perc King, Bill De Alva, Bill Stein

Video #6 Bill Stein, George Moulton, Gene Tate, Earl Swickard, Sam Bame, and Phyl Wallis

Video #7 Phyl Wallis, Buzz Bainbridge, Becky (Bradford) Diven, and John Rogers

Video #35 Old movies from George T. Fike

Phone interviews by Paul Allison.

Letters

Becky Bradford Diven, letters home, 1944–1947

Francoise Ulam to Jae Riebe, anecdotes of the forties and fifties, May 19, 1992

M.J. Poole to Jae Riebe, March 3, 1992

Philip Moon to Sir Rudolf Peierls, April 12, 1992

Virginia Wynne Barella, August 3, 1995

Kyle Wheeler to Deanna Kirby, Pajarito Mountain memories

Kyle Wheeler to Deanna Kirby, memories of Old Blue, February 2, 2000

Documents

Sawyer's Hill Tow Documents, 1944–1948.

Los Alamos Ski Club Newsletters, 1949 to present.

Letters and other documents pertinent to this book supplied by the Los Alamos Ski Club and members.

LASL Community News, June 2, 1960–September 22, 1960.

The Beginning of an Era.

Newspapers

Los Alamos Times

Los Alamos Monitor

Santa Fe New Mexican

LASL Community News

Publications

Badash, Lawrence; Hirschfelder, Joseph O.; Broida, Herbert P. *Reminiscences of Los Alamos, 1943–1945*. D. Reidel Publishing Co. Dordrecht: Holland / Boston: U.S.A. / London: England, 1980.

Brode, Bernice, *Tales of Los Alamos: Life on the Mesa, 1943–1945*. Los Alamos Historical Society, 1997.

Church, Fermor, and Church, Peggy Pond. *Historical Profile: When Los Alamos was a Ranch School*. Los Alamos Historical Society, 1974.

Church, Peggy Pond. *The House at Otowi Bridge*. The University of New Mexico Press, 1959.

Fermi, Laura. *Atoms in the Family: My Life With Enrico Fermi*. University of Chicago Press, 1954.

Hoard, Dorothy. *Los Alamos Outdoors*. Los Alamos Historical Society, 1981.

Jette, Eleanor. *Inside Box 1663*. Los Alamos Historical Society, 1977.

Rhodes, Richard. *The Making of the Atomic Bomb*. Simon and Schuster: New York, 1986.

Russ, Harlow. *Project Alberta: The Preparation of Atomic Bombs for Use in World War II*. Exceptional Books, Ltd., John Allred, publisher, 1990.

Wilson, Jane, and Serber, Charlotte, Eds. *Standing By and Making Do: Women of Wartime Los Alamos*. Los Alamos Historical Society, 1988.

Interviews by Deanna Kirby

Perc King, Hans Bethe, Carol and Stan Moore, Carolyn and Larry Madsen, Bob Kirby, June and Gary Wall, J.O. Johnson, Trish Reed Taylor, Bruce Gavett, Paul Allison, Neil Davis, Jay Wechsler, Ed and Ev Griggs, Hugh Church, Julia Gehre, Becky and Ben Diven, Wes Nichols, John Rogers, Jim "Stretch" Fretwell, John and Elizabeth Orndoff, Jim and Joan Coon, Bill Jarmie, Phyl Wallis, Ginnie Bell, Gene Tate, Bob Watt, Carl Buckland, Dale and Molly Holm, Don Parker, Ivar Lindstrom, Rene Prestwood, Myrna and Ron Strong, Kathy and Milt Gillespie, Inga and Bob Rohwer, Margaret and Harry Flaugh, Nan and Gene Moore, and Markeita and Jim Hedstrom

Part One—The Beginning

The Hill

4 "everyone was there...." Kirby interview
4 "a condemnation proceeding will be instituted" Church and Church, 1974, p. 21
4 "It was like an invasion" Kirby interview
6 "anyone would be crazy to turn down an offer..." Russ, 1984, p. 2
7 "buoyed up by the fact..." Wilson and Serber, 1988, p. 55

Beauty and Grim Reality

7 either in their own cars, with one of the staff. Wilson and Serber, 1988, p. 22
8 "bewitched by the streatches of red earth ..." *LASL Community News*, 6/2/60, p. 6
8 Though some saw only a "hot and barren" country. Rhodes, 1986, p. 451
8 "What a superb retreat.... *LASL Community News*, 6/2/60, p. 6
8 "They were to be a solemn business in our lives." Wilson and Serber, 1988, p. 4
8 "the school furnace was subject to..." Wilson and Serber, 1988, pp. 17–19
9 "Nowhere on the ground was there any sustained greenness." Wilson and Serber, 1988, pp. 36
9 Consumers griped for months. Brode, 1997, p. 24
10 "I think they are just having the excuse to go to Santa Fe." Brode, 1997, p. 25
10 "It made no sense as it was planted by wild nature..." Brode, 1997, p. 11
10 "The soldier left ..." Brode, 1997, p. 11
10 they were "hideous, curvaceous and very black..." Wilson and Serber, 1988, p. 48

10 "we felt powerless under strange circumstances ..." Fermi, 1954, pp. 231–232
11 "It never made of Los Alamos a paradise...." Wilson and Serber, 1988, p. 75
11 "those confounded civilians had a good case." Wilson and Serber, 1988, p. 75
11 That little "ruse" got him elected to the Town Council. Badash et al., 1980, p. 111
12 There were always rumors. Allison video interview.
12 Meanwhile, the Council and Army command wrestled with other issues... *LASL Community News*, 7/28/60, p. 5
12 "It was a Barnum and Bailey World." Wilson and Serber, 1988, p. 51
12 Los Alamos was "plain, utilitarian and quite ugly..." *LASL Community News*, 6/2/60, p. 8
12 "It was a touch of genius to establish our town on the mesa top." *LASL Community News*, 6/2/60, p. 8
13 "What on earth are we hatching here?" *LASL Community News*, 6/16/60, p. 8
13 "What we do here, if we do it, will make a revolution..." *LASL Community News*, 6/16/60, p. 8

Rest and Relaxation

13 "As far as rest and relaxation were concerned..." Allison video interview
13 "We had just about every type of entertainment..." Allison video interview
13 "Theatre No. 2 saw a lot of action..." Allison video interview
13 "The high spot of the show was the end of the last act..." *LASL Community News*, 7/4/60, p. 10
14 "We even had a radio station, KRS." Allison video interview
14 "Lunchtime with Tom and Bob." Allison video interview
14 Party time was synonymous with Saturday nights. *LASL Community News*, 8/11/60, p. 5
14 "Everyone can see if you meesbehave, so ..." *LASL Community News*, 8/11/60, p. 5
14 Conversation among the party goers was highly spirited ... *LASL Community News*, 8/11/60, p. 5
14 Bohr spoke softly, his voice heavily accented. *LASL Community News*, 8/11/60, p. 7
15 His wife stayed in Sweden with their other sons. Rhodes, 1986, p. 473
15 Officially, Bohr's pseudo-name was Nicholas Baker... *LASL Community News*, 8/11/60, p. 5
15 "Even to the big shots, Bohr was a great god." Badash et al., 1980, p. 129
15 When consulting at Los Alamos, the Bohrs were frequent guests. *LASL Community News*, 8/11/60, p. 7
15 The parties were regular social events. Wilson and Serber, 1988, p. 112
15 On Sunday mornings, the whistle was silent. *LASL Community News*, 7/28/60, p. 8
15 "Eight in the car was considered the minimum patriotic load." Wilson and Serber, 1988, p. 111
16 "All you have to do is throw in a line and they bite..." *LASL Community News*, 7/28/60, p. 7
17 But before a shot was fired, the spy escaped. Wilson and Serber, 1988, p. 106
17 Groups of musicians formed ensembles... *LASL Community News*, 7/28/60, p. 6
17 Willie Higinbotham's accordian... *LASL Community News*, 7/28/60, p. 5
17 "He would not take one inch of progress the entire evening." *LASL Community News*, 7/28/60, p. 8
17 "We mostly climbed when I first came." Allison video interview
18 "Jim Coon tried a telemark." Allison video interview

18 "They would need an ambulance..." Wilson and Serber, 1988, p. 96
19 "Even after rousting people all over the mesa, they failed to find a toboggan." Wilson and Serber, 1988, p. 96
19 Someone remembered that there was a doctor at Bruns Hospital in Santa Fe. Wilson and Serber, 1988, p. 97
19 "Poor Dr. Barnett..." Allison video interview
19 "Henry felt he would not survive another trip like that." Wilson and Serber, 1988, p. 97
19 Coon's sense of humor sparkled in his eyes. Kirby interview

Part Two—Sawyer's Hill

The Rope Tow

22 "My gut feeling was I didn't have control of anything." Kirby interview
22 "Immediately, I knew I was going to learn to ski." Kirby interview
22 That was when Davis saw his first submachine gun. Kirby interview
22 "Their warmth helped make life comfortable." Kirby interview
22 "...the pariahs of Los Alamos." Badash et al., 1980, p. 57
22 "I got absolutely nowhere." Badash et al., 1980, p. 57
23 In the beginning, skiing involved a lot of climbing. Kirby interview
23 "close calls with trees falling in unexpected directions." Allison interview
23 "...the explosion cut it as if you had a chain saw." Badash et al., 1980, p. 61
23 "...but so was a hit with an ax." Allison interview and letter, 1986
25 "Los Alamos was really a wonderful place to work." Kirby interview
26 Tyler supported all seven issues raised by Kistiakowsky. Sawyer's Hill Ski Tow Association documents, Tyler, 11/13/44
27 "Many people spent many hours..." Allison video interview
28 Jim Coon thought that the rope tow... Kirby interview
28 "I hauled those containers to the top...." Allison video interview
29 A memo from Nick Metropolis ... explained the problem. Sawyer's Hill Ski Tow Association documents, 1/24/45
29 When the rope broke, it would..." Letter from Poole to Jae Riebe, 3/3/92
29 "People were frantically trying to learn to ski." Allison video interview
29 an afternoon of skiing. Kirby interview
29 Laura Fermi wrote that Enrico was .... Fermi, 1954, p. 225
29 "Rogers was the stud buzzard." Kirby interview
30 "We had a nucleus of ski enthusiasts ...." Kirby interview
30 After Enrico returned home from one of these trips.... Fermi, 1954, p. 225
30 King said that ski trips required strenuous hiking. Kirby interview
30 "I got a couple of ski mobiles...," Badash et al., 1980, p. 61
30 It bogged down, and the skiers had a "weary walk home." Wilson and Serber, 1988, p. 106
30 "We were just so crazy to ski...." Kirby interview

Skiers on the Slopes

31 Jean Bacher recalled that whole families would appear.... Wilson and Serber, 1988, pp. 106–108
31 Laura Fermi would only tackle the lower slope.... Fermi, 1954
31 Brode recalled, "There were always too many trees ...." *LASL Community News*, 1960, p. 8
31 "We had fun in snow...." *LASL Community News*, 1960, p. 8
31 "Bob Walker was the skier to watch...." Kirby interview
31 "King had a physicist's approach to skiing." Allison letter, April 1986
31 "Kisty skied with two skis glued close together." Allison video interview
31 But most agreed that Joan Hinton . . . Allison video interview

31 "She usually came down the slope in one big swoop." Allison video interview
32 Francoise Ulam described Hinton.... Ulam letter to Jae Riebe, 5/19/92
32 Genia Peierls...made her skiing debut at Sawyer's Hill. Jette, 1977, p. 61
32 "That is Russian fatalism!" Allison interview
33 Records indicate she never joined the tow association. Jette, 1977, p. 61
33 "...she did the best she could and was a woman of absolute determination." Kirby interview
33 He quit only when the sun went down.... Fermi, 1954, p. 225
33 Although the tow "was not particularly safe...it lasted the winter." Allison interview, April 1986

The Dawn at Trinity

33 "Every woman had a different idea of what transpired...." Jette, 1977, p. 96
33 When Jette's husband, Eric, departed for Trinity.... Jette, 1977, p. 102
34 "Then it came." *LASL Document/Public Affairs*, LASL-79-78, 1943–1945, pp. 54–56
34 Jette described the moment. Jette, 1977, pp. 103–104
34 Upon the men's return home.... Fermi, 1954, pp. 231–232
34 Oppenheimer would later report.... *LASL Document/Public Affairs*, LASL-79-78, 1943–1945, p. 18
34 "The Great Exodus," as it was called, began in earnest. *LASL Community News*, 12/22/60, p. 5
35 Philip Moon, member of the British Mission, recalled.... Moon letter to Peierls, 4/12/92
35 Brode wrote, "the flashes and bangs...." *LASL Community News*, 8/11/60, p. 8
35 "...never again allow it to be said that the British had no sense of humor." Moon letter to Peierls, 4/12/92
35 The party was "one of the finer moments of the Grand Alliance," Brode wrote. *LASL Community News*, 8/11/60, p. 8
36 "When the light of day was turned on his treachery, I realized he was perfect in his role." Jette, 1977, p. 62
36 "What chance had my kids if the Nazis invaded...with their Russian mother!" Wilson and Serber, 1988, p. 53
36 Bradbury faced the confusion about him with a clear vision of the future. *LASL Document/Public Affairs*, LASL-79-78, p. 62
36 "We've got to keep this place staffed until Congress decides what to do with it." Jette, 1977, p. 111
36 Bradbury would later recall, "In the months following the war the Laboratory struggled...." Rhodes, 1986, p. 755

Tow and Town in Transition

37 Les Seely recalled that he and Kisty had spent a day.... Allison phone interview
37 "The ski tow was getting better and better...." Bradford (later Diven), letter home, 11/8/45
38 "Those heavenly positions...seemed to be in conflict." Bradford (later Diven), letter home, 2/46
38 Brode wrote, "We took the position that is we were short of water...." *LASL Community News*, 9/22/60, p. 6
38 "My faucets were the last to fail...." *LASL Community News*, 9/22/60, p. 6
38 "I found Vermillion worms swimming in my treasured supply," wrote Jane Wilson. Wilson and Serber, 1988, p. 50
38 "Parties were cancelled...the town plunged into a grim and grey period of mourning," wrote Wilson. Wilson and Serber, 1988, pp. 49–50

39 Bulletin notices ordered residents to "boil all water…flush toilets at least once a day for safety." *LASL Community News*, 9/22/60, p. 6

39 "take a water shortage furlough." Kirby interview

39 "Morale dropped to zero," wrote Brode. *LASL Community News*, 9/22/60, p. 7

39 "The Major turned purple with rage…." *LASL Community News*, 9/22/60, p. 7

42 Its sole purpose was to foster skiing at Los Alamos. Los Alamos Ski Club Rules and Regulation, 9/22/48

42 In order for the club to incorporate in the state of New Mexico…. Los Alamos Ski Club minutes, 2/11/47

The Big Snowfall of 1947

44 "It was snowing to beat the band …" Bradford (later Diven), letter home, 12/4/47

44 "You had a lot of handicaps," said Luther Rickerson. Allison video interview

45 "It was a very quiet and grim ride back." Kirby interview

45 "We'd say boots-pass-poles-skis! Boots-pass-poles-skis!" Kirby interview

45 "If you lost the pass while you were skiing…." Allison video interview

45 Once through the back guard gate, cars crawled up four miles…. Allison video interview

45 "I'd load the car with some oil." Allison video interview

45 Glen Waterbury recalled that the tows had to be handcranked. Waterbury letter to Allison, 4/26/86

45 Rickerson said the mail tow was no trouble. Allison video interview

46 "You could almost tell who had cranked it in the morning…." Allison video interview

46 "While the ski club considers Sawyer's Hill to be…." *Los Alamos Times*, 2/13/48

46 The heat went out in all the homes. *Los Alamos Times*, 1/30/48

The First Skiesta

46 "Witnessed by a crowd estimated at 300…. *Los Alamos Times*, 3/5/48

48 In a letter dated May 7, 1948. *Los Alamos Times*, 5/4/48

49 Indeed, the main business of Los Alamos was the Laboratory. *Los Alamos Times*, 7/27/48

50 When Bradbury was asked about the permanence…. *Los Alamos Times*, 7/27/48

50 "When these things are done…." Los Alamos Ski Club Bulletin, 10/24/48

51 "Bainbridge took us to the top of Sawyer's Hill…." Allison interview

51 Supported by the ski club, the ski patrol assumed responsibility…. Kirby interview

51 When the Santa Fe Ski Basin opened for business…. Kirby interview

51 "…a pocketfull of dollars." Allison video interview

51 "It was kind of a thrill coming to Los Alamos….We'd pray we'd get out." Allison video interview

51 "We were impressed with the spirit of the Los Alamos skiers." Allison video interview

51 Five years of bonanza snowfalls. *Santa Fe New Mexican*, 12/20/55

51 "This is the way we cut slopes at Sawyer's." Kirby interview

52 "It was a little scary." Allison video interview

52 One slope that was cleared quickly…. Allison video interview

52 "I remember night skiing only once...." Kirby interview

52 "In those days we didn't have safety bindings…." Barela letter to Kirby, 8/3/95

52 "It was so cold and the bumps became holes…." Kirby interview

52 "Bill Jarmie yodeling as he went flying down the mountain." Allison video interview

53 Rocks were a frequent hazard. Allison video interview
53 "The slope faced east." Kirby interview
53 "We...knew there was something up there." Kirby interview
53 "We had to confirm the snow conditions ourselves." Allison video interview
53 "We were astonished at its potential as a ski area." Allison video interview
54 "There was nearly four feet of snow, and we hadn't skied at Sawyer's for nearly a month." Kirby interview
54 "That was discovery day...there was snow at Pajarito." Kirby interview
54 Gene Tate, the ski club president at the time, was least enthusiastic. Kirby interview
55 Fretwell thought it was surprising easy.... Kirby interview
55 "It seems to me...it was a resounding vote in favor of doing that." Allison video interview
55 "A nucleus of people decided.... They were highly motivated and got things done." Allison video interview

Part Three—Pajarito Mountain

Pajarito Mountain: The Move

Video interviews of Bob Thorn, John Ordoff, and Bill Jarmie conducted by Allison et al. Rene Prestwood, Dale Holm, and John Rogers interviewed by Kirby.

The Story of Camp May Road

Video interviews of Tom Putnam and Bob Thorn by Allison et al. Interviews of Dale Holm, John Rogers, and Stretch Fretwell conducted by Kirby.

59 The *Santa Fe New Mexican*, September 19, 1957

"Skiers of the Hill, Arise!"

Video interview of Bob Thorn by Allison et al. Interviews of John Rogers, Stretch Fretwell, Dale Holm, and Carl Buckland conducted by Kirby.

Growing Pains for Los Alamos

67 The enrollment for the public schools was 4,078 childen. *LASL Community News*, January 28, 1960.
68 Paul Wilson...estimated that the housing shortage.... *LASL Community News*, December 18, 1959.
68 Even the future of Ashley Pond was being pondered. *LASL Community News*, May 21, 1959.

Saga of the Rope Tows

Interviews of Dale Holm, Bob Rohwer, Kyle Wheeler, Rene Prestwood, Wes Nichols, John Rogers, J.O. Johnson, Bill Jarmie, Joan Coon, Phyl Wallis, and Don Parker by Kirby.

Rocognition

75 "Club of the Month," *Southwestern Skier*, January 1960

Blueprint for Pajarito

Video interview of Bob Thorn by Allison et al. Interview of John Orndoff by Kirby.

The Second Ski Lodge

Interviews of John Rogers, Stretch Fretwell, Carl Buckland, J.O. Johnson conducted by Kirby.

The Cafeteria

Interviews of Stretch Fretwell and Julia Gehre conducted by Kirby.

Fireplace

Interviews of J.O. Johnson, Larry Madsen, and Carolyn Madsen by Kirby.

The T-Bar

Interviews of Ron Strong, Stretch Fretwell, John Orndoff, Rene Prestwood, Bob Thorn, J.O. Johnson, Don Parker, Ivar Lindstrom, Bob Rohwer, Harry Flaugh, and Bob Kirby conducted by Kirby.

82 In a proposal to the ski club board.... Memo from Stretch Fretwell, Chairman of the Lift Committee: Proposal for Ski Lift at Pajarito Mountain, February 1, 1962.

Future for the Ski Area

Interviews of Don Parker, John Orndoff, Bob Rohwer, Margaret Flaugh, J.O. Johnson, Milt Gillespie, Harry Flaugh, and Ed and Ev Griggs by Kirby.

87 Gordon Smith, Los Alamos Ski Club president, newsletter to members, October 18, 1963

88 Los Alamos Ski Club memos, 1965, regarding popularity of the area and possible expansion

Shaping the Ski Slopes

Interviews of Bob Thorn, Stretch Fretwell, Rene Prestwood, Larry Madsen, Harry Flaugh, Ron Strong, Margaret Flaugh, Markeita Hedstrom, Bob Rohwer, Kyle Wheeler, Carolyn Madsen, and Jim Hedstrom by Kirby.

Rocks and Stumps

Interviews of Milt Gillespie, J.O. Johnson, Kathy Gillespie, Bob Rohwer, and Stan Moore by Kirby.

What's in a Name?

Interviews of Stretch Fretwell, Bob Thorn, Rene Prestwood, Ron Strong, Milt Gillespie, Harry Flaugh, Gene Moore, Nan Moore, Larry Madsen, Kathy Gillespie, and Markeita Hedstrom by Kirby.

The "New" Lodge

117 Letter to the editor from Judy Young, *Los Alamos Monitor,* 1987

Interviews of Gary Wall, Larry Madsen, Harry Flaugh, Markeita Hedstrom, and June Wall by Kirby.

"Old Blue"

Interviews of Kyle Wheeler, Harry Flaugh, Ron Strong, and Larry Madsen by Kirby.

Pajarito Mountain Spared by the Cerro Grande Fire

Interview of Bruce Gavett by Kirby.

Photo credits

The photographs used in this book were used with the permission of the listed individuals and organizations. Where only one person or organization is identified on a page with multiple photos, all photos on that page are courtesy that person or organization.

viii	L.D.P. King
Part 1	
2	L.D.P. King
4	Los Alamos Historical Society
5	Los Alamos Historical Society
6	Los Alamos Historical Society
7	Los Alamos Historical Society
8	photo of buildings around pond courtesy Stretch Fretwell; other photos Los Alamos National Laboratory
9	Los Alamos Historical Society, photo of Sundt apartment courtesy Carl Buckland
10	Los Alamos Historical Society
11	Los Alamos Historical Society
12	Los Alamos National Laboratory
13	Los Alamos Historical Society
14	Los Alamos National laboratory
15	Carl Buckland (people in truck); unknown
16	Carl Buckland
17	L.D.P. King
18	Los Alamos Historical Society, large photo; L.D.P. King
19	L.D.P. King
Part 2	
20	John Orndoff
22	Los Alamos Historical Society
23	Los Alamos National Laboratory
24	Los Alamos Ski Club
25	Los Alamos National Laboratory
26	John Orndoff
27	Ben Diven
28	L.D. Rickerson
29	Paul Allison
30	Carl Buckland; Los Alamos Ski Club
31	Unknown; L.D.P. King
33	Ben Diven
35	Los Alamos Historical Society
36	Los Alamos Historical Society
37	Los Alamos National Laboratory
38	Los Alamos Historical Society
40	L.D.P. King
42	Los Alamos National Laboratory
43	Unknown
46	Becky Bradford Diven
47	Los Alamos Ski Club
48	Los Alamos Ski Club
49	Jim Coon
50	John Orndoff
51	John Orndoff
52	John Orndoff
53	Dale Holm

54 John Orndoff
55 Phyllis Wallis

Part 3
56 Roger White
58 Los Alamos National Laboratory
61 Los Alamos National Laboratory
62 Los Alamos National Laboratory
63 Dale Holm
64 Dale Holm
68 Los Alamos National Laboratory
69 Los Alamos Ski Club
70 Los Alamos Ski Club
71 Dale Holm
72 Trish Lester
73 Los Alamos National Laboratory
74 Bob Rohwer
75 Trish Lester
76 Dale Holm
79 Roger White
80 Paul Allison
82 Los Alamos National Laboratory
83 Los Alamos National Laboratory
85 Paul Allison
86 Los Alamos Ski Club
87 John Orndoff
88 J.O. Johnson
90 Tom Scolman
92 Harry Flaugh
93 Larry Madsen
94 Carolyn Madsen
95 photo of Thorn courtesy John Orndoff; photo of Flaugh courtesy Larry Madsen
97 Margaret Flaugh
98 photo of Moore courtesy Harry Flaugh; photo of Flaugh and Strong courtesy Margaret Flaugh
99 Carolyn Madsen
100 Harry Flaugh
101 Larry Madsen
103 Margaret Flaugh
104 Harry Flaugh
106 photos 1 & 2 courtesy Lorraine Thorn; photos 3 & 4 courtesy Gloria Sharp; photo 5 courtesy Dale Holm; photo 6 courtesy Carolyn Madsen
108 Tom Scolman; Carolyn Madsen
109 Bill Chambers; Bob Kirby
110 Harry Flaugh
111 Nancy Thorn
113 Robert Thorn
114 Bill Chambers
115 Bill Chambers
116 Margaret Flaugh; Robert Thorn
118 top photo Harry Flaugh; lower photo Carolyn Madsen
119 top photo Paul Allison; lower photo Larry Madsen
120 Bruce Gavett
121 Dale Holm